T0381444

DRAINS & RADIATORS
A guide to business and life

Master the art of identifying, filtering
and ultimately surrounding yourself with
the right people to grow your business
and enhance your life

Neil Jenkinson & Victoria Johnson

authorHOUSE®

AuthorHouse™
1663 Liberty Drive
Bloomington, IN 47403
www.authorhouse.com
Phone: 833-262-8899

Published by AuthorHouse 09/25/2024

ISBN: 979-8-8230-3479-1 (sc)
ISBN: 979-8-8230-3478-4 (e)

Print information available on the last page.

ABOUT THE AUTHORS

Neil Jenkinson and Victoria Johnson bring a wealth of experience and insight to their latest book, drawing from their diverse backgrounds in marketing and psychology to offer readers a fresh perspective on human behaviour.

Neil Jenkinson

Neil Jenkinson is a dynamic marketing consultant who has honed his craft at some of the world's most prestigious agency groups. His journey began on the client side at Cadbury's Schweppes, where he quickly became captivated by the dynamic world of marketing agencies. During a decade-long tenure at The Marketing Store Worldwide in London and Paris, Neil discovered the power of the Myers-Briggs personality assessment—a tool that revolutionised his understanding of human interaction. With this framework, Neil mastered the art of navigating both personal and professional relationships, optimising his interactions to manage the "drains and radiators" of human behaviour.

In 2003, Neil launched his own collaborative agency, eventually joining forces with the Ogilvy Group to bring innovative marketing solutions to a diverse client base. His journey has taken him across the globe, from McCann in the UK to TIS Group in Croatia, where he has witnessed firsthand how different personalities can shape a company's culture and performance.

Victoria Johnson

Victoria Johnson is the visionary founder of a cutting-edge digital marketing agency where the fusion of psychology and business strategy creates transformative results. Armed with a degree in psychology, Victoria possesses a profound understanding of the psychological triggers that influence decision-making in today's "Drains & Radiators" culture. Her curiosity about human interaction led her to a distinguished career in education, where she spent over a decade as the Head of the Psychology Department, igniting a passion for the subject in her students.

After twelve years in academia, Victoria transitioned into the private sector, where she skilfully applies her psychological expertise to solve real-world challenges. Her ability to craft compelling marketing campaigns that resonate with audiences on a deep level has made her an influential figure in the industry.

THE BOOK

In their groundbreaking book, Neil and Victoria delve into the intricacies of human behaviour in both professional and social settings, exploring the profound impact individuals can have on each other. They offer practical strategies for enhancing influence while safeguarding mental and physical well-being. By combining their extensive knowledge of psychology and marketing, Neil and Victoria provide readers with valuable insights to navigate the complexities of human interaction in today's fast-paced world, helping them become more self-aware of their own "Drains and Radiators" traits.

CONTENTS

INTRODUCTION TO DRAINS & RADIATORS

We're all born drains,
but flourish we must

t's Sunday 21 August 2011, there's a live interview conducted by Adam Jacques of The Independent with the legendary guitarist, producer, and one half of The Eurhythmics Dave Stewart. He is regarded as one of the major figures in the UK pop culture, but he also has interesting life lessons, and that's when I heard the 'drains & radiators' quote for the first time:

How do you deal with negativity?

I always remember what my mum told me when I was about seven, but it really only clicked in later. She said, 'there are two kinds of people, drains and radiators. Make sure you keep clear of the drains.'

In life, there are drains and radiators. It's a phrase my mum always said: some people will suck the air right out of the room, while others come in and everything feels sunny. It's why I like to make sure I'm surrounded by radiators, or at least make sure the radiators are not outweighed by drains.

This stuck in my head for, well, forever! It's never left me, in fact from that day, I adopted it as my own mantra for life. It's been an inspiration in business and something that has guided me through life simply because it's so true. People really do fall into the category of being a drain or a radiator, but there's a caveat; it's a personal perception. An individual that falls into either category may only be relevant to you. In other words, that person who you consider a drain, someone who is sapping your energy and sucking the life out of your business and stopping you from reaching your true potential, might be a radiator to someone else. And that's what makes this Drains & Radiator philosophy so difficult to navigate, people can have both traits, swapping & changing depending on their situation or environment, and some people just display one trait all of the time. We call these pure drains or pure radiators, more on these later in this book.

We are all born drains. We rely on our mothers to feed and nurture us. It is often said that babies are born learning, but what are they really capable of picking up on? What about something as subtle as their parents' emotions? While infants vary in their sensitivity, research shows that babies do, indeed, sense and react to their parents' emotional cues. Generally speaking, they pick up on what their parents are giving off.

"From birth, infants pick up on emotional cues from others. Even very young infants look to caregivers to determine how to react to a given situation," says Jennifer E. Lansford, PhD, a professor with the Social Science Research Institute and the Centre for Child and Family Policy at Duke University.

Together with all parts of brain development, (physical, cognitive, language, etc.) a baby's emotional development begins early, and babies look to their parents' emotional responses to help them interpret and react to the world around them. Studies have shown that infants as young as one month-old sense when a parent is depressed or angry and are affected by the parent's mood.

Understanding that even infants are affected by adult emotions can help parents do their best in supporting their child's healthy development. Parents and caregivers who express positive emotions and who respond to babies' needs in a positive and loving manner are helping promote feelings of security in their child, and these are the earliest signs of creating radiator-like qualities. But it's important to remember that we can not classify children into drains and radiators; they are all dependent on their parents for the basic physiological and safety needs (nutrition and water, access to fresh air, rest and exercise plus security and feeling safe etc.) as famously outlined in Maslow's Hierarchy of Needs. So, we must exclude children and any adults with disabilities that justify dependency from other adults, we can't simply label them as drains.

It is not uncommon for us to see quotes about 'Drains and Radiators' reminding us to choose who we surround ourselves with; these quotes have been around for decades. Typical advice given by people using these quotes will state: Avoid drains and stay close to radiators; if only it was that simple.

The most common phraseology used is that radiators cheer you up, they exude warmth, comfort, positivity, smiles and encouragement. By contrast, drains bring you down, they are dark and cold, miserable, moany and suck your life and energy. In business, these traits can also mean the difference between becoming a profitable business with a can-do attitude versus a loss-making business where there no camaraderie.

But how often, when you hear or see any Drains & Radiator quote, do *you* stop and reflect on which one you are? How often do you stop and question whether you drain or radiate those around you in business or life? Self-reflection is difficult and it can be tough to accept that we aren't always what or who we would like to be, however, self-reflection is key to being the best that you can possibly be.

Yes, it is important to check who you surround yourself with, but it is also important to check how people around you are feeling in your company. Are you radiating warmth and energy to those around you? Are you sharing in the excitement of their achievements? Are you providing them with that reassurance and support that helps them fulfil their dreams? Are you the person that people come to when they have good news to share?

Are you a Radiator or Drain: The Power of Contagious Happiness

Are you spreading joy or sapping energy? This is the crucial question posed by Dr Andy Cope, a leading expert in happiness and positive psychology, and the author of The Art of Being Brilliant. In May 2024, Dr Cope unveiled his groundbreaking research on what he calls the "Two-Percenters"—the happiest individuals in the world, who represent just 2% of the population. Unlike most psychologists, who focus on mental illness, Dr Cope was captivated by the positive end of the wellbeing spectrum. His revolutionary idea: what if, instead of examining mental illness, we studied positivity and wellness?

That's precisely what Dr Cope set out to do. He conducted surveys to assess people's happiness levels and plotted their results on a wellbeing chart. Broadly speaking, most people in developed countries occupy the "perfectly fine" zone. We generally have decent health, a roof over our heads, a fridge stocked with food, and a comfortable bed. In terms of happiness, most of us are "mildly happy most of the time."

However, in recent years, the pace of change has accelerated dramatically. Climate emergencies, social media, technology, algorithms, neurodiversity, epidemics, pandemics, artificial intelligence, fake news, wars—these challenges have left even those who were "perfectly fine" running on empty. Before long, low-level negativity creeps in, and a third of the population finds itself in a zone characterised by background grumbling and tutting.

It's important to note that Dr Cope is not talking about individuals with clinical issues. Those exist at the very bottom of the chart, in what he calls the "danger zone." Instead, he refers to those who possess a special talent for dragging others down with a well-aimed negative remark— what we often call emotional drains.

We've all encountered them. The people who make you wish for a Netflix-style "Skip Intro" button for conversations. These individuals brighten up a room simply by leaving it. Dr Cope calls this state "languishing," and those who dwell in this negative zone are aptly named dementors, energy vampires, mood hoovers—or, simply, drains.

The Radiator Effect: 40% Extra Happiness

Most of us would prefer to reside at the opposite end of the wellbeing spectrum, which is why Dr Cope turned psychology on its head and focused on the Two-Percenters—those who sit at the very top of the wellbeing chart.

He coined the term "two-percenters" to highlight their rarity. These individuals possess 30% more happiness and 40% more energy than their draining counterparts. They are the radiators—the ones who exude happiness, the flourishing few who are genuinely living their best lives. Dr Cope's research aimed to uncover three key insights:

Who are these people who feel amazing on a regular basis?
What are they doing that enables them to flourish?
Most importantly, what can we learn from them to improve our own mental wealth?

In essence, Dr Cope embarked on this research for personal reasons. He wanted to understand the secret to the Two-Percenters' zest for life—so he could become one himself!

The Good News: The Ripple Effect of Radiating Happiness

There are two significant pieces of good news about being a Two-Percenter. First, and most obviously, being your "best self" more often—which is essentially what it means to be a Two-Percenter—will fundamentally transform your life, both at work and at home. In Two-Percenter mode, you'll be happier, more creative, resilient, positive, and energetic.

The second, and perhaps best news, is that feeling amazing has tremendous side effects. Human emotions are contagious. When you're operating at your best, you create an emotional uplift in those around you. So, being a Two-Percenter is not only good for you; it also has a positive impact on your family, friends, colleagues, neighbours, and community.

If emotions are indeed contagious (and they undoubtedly are!), the big question is: what are people catching from you?

The bottom line is simple. Whether you're a radiator or a drain will drastically affect not only your own life but also the lives of those closest to you. As Dr Cope wisely advises: "You can drag people up, or you can take them down. My advice? Join the ranks of the Two-Percenters—and pass it on!"

Beware of The Drains, they're around every corner!

We don't believe that anyone sets out to be a drain; people don't wake up in the morning determined to drain the positive energy from people. So how does this happen?

If we are honest with ourselves, we can probably all admit that at some point we have been the drain on others. We all have occasions where our conversations and language have been mainly negative, the glass half empty, the huffing and puffing and sighing as we moan about how badly life is treating us. Becoming a drain is what happens when we get stuck. We get angry, and frustrated, and we may get feelings of stress or depression and whilst it affects us it also affects those around us.

This is why it is important not to get stuck in 'the curve' and why it is important to check where you are in the curve and if your behaviour is draining others. The change curve is a popular model that is used to understand the stages of personal transition and organisational change. In the workplace, the change curve can help predict how employees will react to change, such as switching teams or allocation of new roles or responsibilities, in general life, it the change curve can explain how we react to changes and new situations.

The change curve is based on a model of the five stages of grief–denial, anger, bargaining, depression and acceptance– originally described by Elisabeth Kübler-Ross in her 1969 book On Death and Dying. Since then, the stages have been utilised and adapted into the Kübler-Ross change curve, which individuals and organisations alike use to help people understand their reactions to significant change or loss.

While there are numerous versions of the curve and individuals may react differently based on personality and experience, most change curve models follow this general pattern:

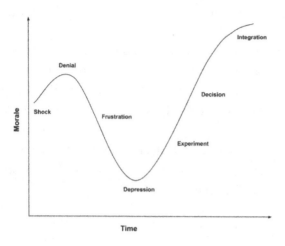

Fig 1: Kübler-Ross change curve

Stage 1: Shock

When a change is first introduced, people's first reaction is usually shock as they respond to the challenge to their status quo. In the workplace, this short-lived stage of shock can result in a loss of productivity due to a lack of information or fear of the unknown. In life, shock typically results in a break in routine.

Stage 2: Denial

After the initial shock has passed, people commonly experience denial. Employees typically question why the change is needed and some convince themselves and others, that the change won't happen or won't affect them. There may be a temporary return to normality, but this is usually short lived.

Stage 3: Frustration or anger

Anger or frustration often follows shock and denial. Individuals may begin to feel fear and start to assign blame. Performance levels start to drop during this phase and routine is completely disrupted. This is when drain or radiator traits manifest themselves with some people clearly fighting change as their personal revolt whilst others endeavouring to remain positive and provide support and communication to others.

Stage 4: Depression

The lowest point of the change curve, when morale is at its lowest, comes when the anger begins to wear off. Typically, individuals realise that the change is inevitable and this translate into the depression stage where energy levels are commonly low, and self-doubt and anxiety levels can peak.

Stage 5: Experiment

At this stage, people begin to accept the situation as they test and explore what the changes mean to them. While some may accept the change because they are forced to, others may learn to embrace the change positively. For radiators, this is an easy adoption but drains need more coercion. During this phase, overall productivity begins to improve.

Stage 6: Decision

In the decision stage, productivity continues to rise as people continue to learn how to work in a changed environment or in life, simply start to accept change and ultimately embrace it.

Stage 7: Integration

At this final stage, the change is now normalised, and it becomes part of the new status quo. We can use this cycle of change to inform our decisions and responses the next time we face any new transition.

The Kübler-Ross change curve is important because it amplifies the traits we all have in our drain vs radiator equilibrium. When people start to display drain-like behaviour this may be a sign that they are stuck in the change curve. It is part of the relationship for us to help them recognise their behaviour and support them to move on. Whilst it is down to the individual to want to change, this does require self-reflection, which can often be difficult if we are in a negative mindset. That's where friends and family can support us in seeing this.

Yes, we should surround ourselves with radiators, but we should also be radiators to the drains.

Tips for Business and Life:

Change is inevitable, but getting stuck in its emotional stages can be a real obstacle. If you or a colleague find yourselves caught in the grips of the change curve, it's crucial to have strategies that help move things forward to the Decision and Integration stages swiftly. Often, it's the

Frustration or Depression stages that tend to linger, causing the most harm. Addressing these stages with empathetic conversations can make a world of difference.

Here's how you can help yourself or others:

Ask Questions: Start by opening up a dialogue. Ask questions like, "How do you feel about this?" or "How is this affecting you?" This not only shows empathy but also helps identify the core issues. Encourage reflection with questions like, "What actions might you take to start healing?"

Probe Deeper: Once the conversation begins, delve deeper by asking, "What might change as a result of these actions?" and "What's the quickest path forward?" Offering support is vital, so ask, "What can I do to help you?"

Nurture Growth: Collaborate on a plan of action. Ask, "Can we create a plan together?" and suggest periodic reviews with, "Why don't we check in on this plan midway?" Make sure they are comfortable by asking, "How do you feel about this plan?"

Implementing these simple steps can transform negative thoughts into positive actions. Whether you're dealing with a colleague exhibiting Drain-like qualities or if you're stuck in the Frustration stage yourself, remember that asking, probing, and nurturing can lead to radiator-like improvements.

REDEFINING MASLOW'S HIERARCHY OF NEEDS

From 1943 to Today —
How Far We've Come

n 1943, Abraham Maslow introduced a groundbreaking idea that would shape our understanding of human motivation for decades. His hierarchy of needs, a staple in psychology, offered a way to categorize and prioritize human desires, ranging from the most basic survival instincts to the pursuit of self-fulfilment. But oh, how we've changed since then. The world today is a far cry from the one Maslow knew—our motivations are more complex, our needs more nuanced, and our challenges, both personal and professional, far more intricate.

Let's take a quick refresher on Maslow's original theory from his paper, "A Theory of Human Motivation." Maslow's hierarchy, while revolutionary for its time, reflected a simpler era. The theory is often depicted as a pyramid, though Maslow himself didn't present it that way. This pyramid became a symbol of the idea that human needs build upon each other, starting with the most basic physiological needs at the bottom and moving up toward self-actualization at the top.

Fig 2: Maslow's hierarchy of needs (original version)

Maslow's hierarchy has been used widely as both a psychological idea and a practical tool in various fields, from education and healthcare to management and social work. It's been a framework to understand how people are motivated to achieve their goals, but it's also been criticized for being too rigid, too linear, and not reflective of the dynamic and interconnected nature of human needs.

So, how does Maslow's theory hold up in today's world? And what happens when we apply it to our understanding of "drains" and "radiators"—those who sap energy and those who radiate success?

The Need for a 21ˢᵗ-Century Update

While Maslow's hierarchy has served as a valuable guide for understanding human motivation, the rapid evolution of society, technology, and psychology demands a fresh perspective. The world has changed, and so too must our frameworks for understanding it. Critics have pointed out several key limitations in Maslow's original model:

Our Needs Are Dynamic

Maslow suggested that one must satisfy lower-level needs before progressing to higher ones. But we now understand that human needs are not always linear or hierarchical. Today's fast-paced world, with its constant demands and distractions, means people often pursue multiple needs simultaneously or in a different order than the hierarchy suggests. The idea that we must patiently climb a ladder to self-actualization feels outdated in a world where immediacy is the norm.

Cultural Bias

Maslow's hierarchy was based on Western ideals, particularly the focus on individualism and self-actualization. However, in our increasingly multicultural society, different cultures may prioritize community, social connectedness, or spiritual fulfilment over individual achievement. This cultural bias limits the hierarchy's applicability across diverse populations.

Lack of Empirical Grounding

Maslow's theory has faced criticism for its lack of strong empirical evidence. While the hierarchy provides a useful framework, its strict ordering of needs isn't always supported by research. In practice, it's more useful to view the hierarchy as a descriptive, rather than prescriptive, model—one that can be adapted to the complexities of modern life.

Embracing Technology of Today

Today's digital technology offers unprecedented tools to refine our understanding of Maslow's Hierarchy of Needs. With access to vast amounts of data, we can analyse human behaviour and motivation on a scale unimaginable in Maslow's time. Social media platforms, wearable devices, and online communities provide insights into how individuals seek and fulfil their needs in real-time, revealing nuances in how safety, belonging, and self-actualisation manifest.

Additionally, artificial intelligence and machine learning enable personalised experiences, helping us understand and address unmet needs more effectively. By leveraging these technologies, we can adapt Maslow's model to better reflect the complexities of contemporary life, offering a more dynamic framework for understanding human motivation today.

Bringing Maslow's Hierarchy Into the 21st Century

To remain relevant, Maslow's hierarchy needs a makeover— one that reflects the realities of our time. This updated model should incorporate contemporary challenges like the digital revolution, multicultural interactions, and the blurred lines between work and personal life. By modernising the hierarchy, we can create a more accurate and useful tool for understanding human motivation today.

Here's how we might rethink each level of Maslow's pyramid for the 21st century:

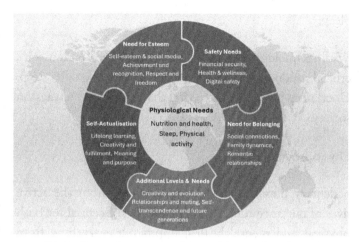

Fig 3: Our take on a modernised hierarchy of needs

Physiological Needs: Beyond Survival

In today's world, physiological needs are about more than just survival. They include the quality and sustainability of what we consume, the impact of our lifestyles on our health, and the challenges posed by modern technology.

Nutrition and Health:

We now know that what we eat affects not just our bodies, but our minds as well. Encouraging balanced diets rich in essential nutrients can greatly enhance mental and emotional wellbeing.

Sleep:

With technology disrupting our natural sleep patterns, it's crucial to educate people on the importance of quality sleep. Good sleep hygiene is more vital than ever in our always-on society.

Physical Activity:

Sedentary lifestyles are a stark departure from the active lives of our ancestors. Regular exercise is essential for both physical and mental health, improving everything from mood to cognitive function.

Safety Needs: Modern Anxieties

Today's safety concerns go beyond physical security to include financial stability, data privacy, and navigating an unpredictable global landscape.

Financial Security:

In an era of economic uncertainty, job security and financial planning are top concerns. Addressing these fears is key to reducing anxiety and promoting wellbeing.

Health and Wellness:

Global health challenges like pandemics, climate change, and food security reshape how we think about safety.

Mental health awareness and rapid medical advancements are crucial components of this new safety net.

Digital Safety:

In the digital age, protecting personal data and privacy is paramount. Understanding the psychological impact of online threats is an essential part of modern therapy.

Need for Belonging: Connection in the Digital Age

The need for love and belonging remains crucial, but the ways we connect have changed dramatically with the advent of social media and online communities.

Social Connections:

While the internet can foster connections, it can also lead to feelings of isolation. Helping people navigate these digital relationships is vital.

Family Dynamics:

The concept of family is evolving, and so too are the dynamics within it. Therapy must adapt to these changes, helping individuals find belonging in diverse family structures.

Romantic Relationships:

The landscape of dating and marriage is more complex than ever. Understanding the nuances of modern relationships is key to fostering intimacy and trust.

Need for Esteem: Balancing Recognition and Authenticity

In a world where external validation is just a click away, finding a balance between recognition and self-worth is a delicate task.

Self-Esteem and Social Media:

Social media can skew self-perception, making it crucial to help individuals develop genuine self-esteem independent of online personas.

Achievement and Recognition:

The pressure to achieve can lead to burnout. Encouraging healthy ambition while promoting internal validation is essential.

Respect and Freedom:

Discussions about respect and personal freedom are central to today's social discourse. Understanding these needs in the context of modern society is vital for wellbeing.

Self-Actualization: A Continuous Journey

Self-actualization remains the pinnacle of human motivation, but in today's world, it's a lifelong journey rather than a final destination.

Lifelong Learning:

In a rapidly changing world, the pursuit of knowledge is ongoing. Encouraging a mindset of continuous growth helps individuals adapt and thrive.

Creativity and Fulfilment:

Helping people find creative outlets and personal fulfilment is crucial for self-actualization. This pursuit can lead to profound growth and satisfaction.

Meaning and Purpose:

In a complex world, finding meaning is more challenging than ever. Guiding individuals toward what truly matters to them is key to achieving self-actualization.

Expanding the Hierarchy: Beyond the Individual

As we rethink Maslow's hierarchy, it's important to consider additional layers that reflect the complexities of modern life, such as relationships, creativity, and self-transcendence.

Relationships and Mating:

Building and maintaining relationships is fundamental to human behavior. Recognizing the importance of these connections is crucial in understanding motivation.

Self-Transcendence:

Going beyond self-actualization, self-transcendence involves connecting with something greater than oneself. This level of consciousness can profoundly impact how individuals approach life and interact with others.

A Final Thought: Embracing Complexity for a Radiant Future

Updating Maslow's hierarchy isn't just about keeping up with the times; it's about embracing the complexity of human needs in a way that reflects our current reality. As mental health professionals, educators, or leaders, our goal is to guide individuals toward fulfilling lives that balance personal needs with the greater good.

By integrating modern insights into this timeless framework, we can better understand human behaviour, foster wellbeing, and create a society filled with radiators—those who not only seek fulfilment but also inspire and uplift others. Let's continue our journey toward a more compassionate, connected, and radiant world with far less drains.

Our hope is that this revised version becomes more relevant to us, with a focus on making the content relatable to contemporary readers while retaining the essential ideas of the original text. In doing so, we can gain a far deeper understanding as to how *and* why people display drain-like traits and understanding can be the catalyst to making a change for good.

Tips for Business and Life:

In our fast-paced and interconnected world, understanding the complexity of human needs is more crucial than ever. Building on Maslow's foundational ideas, we can embrace a more nuanced framework that reflects today's realities. Here's a guide to help you and others move towards fulfilling, balanced lives:

1. **Prioritise Well-Being**

Ensure that basic physical and emotional needs are met, as these are the foundation for all higher-level aspirations. Encourage regular self-care practices and mental health support within your community or organisation.

Tip: Schedule regular check-ins with yourself and your team to assess physical health, emotional well-being, and work-life balance. Encourage breaks and offer resources for mental health support.

2. Foster Authentic Connections

Promote a sense of belonging by creating inclusive and supportive environments. Cultivate relationships that are genuine and meaningful, encouraging collaboration and open communication.

Tip: Organise team-building activities and community events that allow people to connect on a deeper level. Encourage empathy and active listening in all interactions.

3. Encourage Growth and Learning

Support personal and professional development by providing opportunities for continuous learning and skill enhancement. Empower individuals to pursue their passions and explore new interests.

Tip: Offer workshops, training sessions, and mentorship programs that cater to diverse interests and career goals. Celebrate achievements and milestones to motivate ongoing growth.

4. Inspire Purpose and Contribution

Help individuals find purpose by aligning their personal values with their work and community involvement. Encourage them to contribute to the greater good, inspiring others through their actions.

Tip: Create initiatives that allow people to participate in meaningful projects, such as volunteer programs or sustainability efforts. Recognise and reward contributions that have a positive impact on the community and beyond.

5. Cultivate a Radiant Environment

Aim to be a radiator—someone who uplifts and inspires those around them. Encourage positivity, resilience, and a forward-thinking mindset, reducing negativity and drain-like behaviours.

Tip: Lead by example, demonstrating optimism and adaptability. Encourage problem-solving and creative thinking, focusing on solutions rather than obstacles.

By integrating these modern insights into your personal and professional life, you can help create a compassionate, connected, and radiant world. This approach not only aligns with contemporary needs but also retains the essential elements of Maslow's original framework, fostering a deeper understanding of human behaviour and the potential for positive change.

Friends in peril – a change for good?

To illustrate our ambition, we dug out an extract from US Magazine Psychology Today. In 2013, Friendship Doctor Irene S Levine Ph.D. published My Friend Is Draining Me!

Posted October 5, 2013

Question:

Hi Irene,

My BFF and I have been friends since high school (I am now 26). For most of these years we have been as tight and as happy as you could imagine. However, I feel she has been relying on me too heavily for emotional support and empathy while ignoring any issues I may be going through.

She has complained about her now ex for years, cheated on him last year, broke up with him this year, and one week after they broke up hooked up with someone new (her ex and her were together nearly 9 years). I have been secret keeper and confidante through all of this. Meanwhile, I went through some issues over the past few years, like my brother being hospitalized for a few months after a schizophrenic break, and I get next to nothing. Sometimes I have told her something I was feeling that was really important and she has said nothing!

I am in no way perfect or always right but frequently this friend uses me for an emotional bouncing board. She has told me before she finds it hard to be empathetic towards me but I feel I am expected to hear her out on everything. She has even spoken to me about suicide before. I feel this pressure to assist her and the lack of reciprocation has damaged our relationship and I don't know how to fix it. Help!

Furthermore, my personal emotional well-being is damaged because of it. I sometimes feel I am having a fantastic day or been on a great date and she will call and bring me way down. No answer is ever enough. Just listening is never enough. I feel like a sponge that soaks up all the negativity and misery she feels. Some of these issues I feel she has brought on herself. And her messing around has complicated things with the rest of my friends.

Furthermore, and perhaps the largest issue, is if I ignore her, I feel guilty—and it doesn't work anyway because even if I do not prompt her, she will spill everything to me. I love this girl to death, I could never ditch her; I just don't know how to manage living my life the way I want without being dragged into her drama but still maintaining the relationship.

This situation has made me unbelievably sad. It is not that I don't want her to tell me important things, it is just I don't want that to be it. A lot of the time, we will go out for a girls' night and it will end with her crying. This has been going on for a while and it is becoming very difficult to navigate. I feel I am becoming angry and frustrated with her something I never wanted to feel.

Perhaps my expectations of her are unfair? I am a very sensitive, understanding person but I just don't know what to do and feel I have nothing more to offer her, and am falling into bitterness and resentment, feelings I am very uncomfortable with.

Thank you for your support and sorry if this sounds desperate.

Marissa

Answer:

Hi Marissa,

Even though this relationship has become one-sided and has reached the point where it feels draining, you sound like a sensitive and caring friend. Moreover, your note makes it clear you value this friendship and want to preserve it.

If your friend is crying, bringing you down, and talking about suicide, there is a high likelihood that she is depressed. When someone is depressed, that individual's world shrinks considerably, and the person may be so self-involved that she doesn't have the capacity to be as caring and empathetic as you or she would like her to be.

It sounds like your friend is just managing to tread water. Feeling sad, angry, resentful, frustrated, and desperate like you do under these circumstances is normal.

Both to help your friend and to preserve your friendship, you need to strongly suggest that she seek professional help. Reassure her that you really care about her, but see her floundering and can't provide the kind or amount of help she needs. Raise the possibility, explicitly, that she may be depressed and do some homework so you are able to suggest a therapist or organization in your community.

Right now, she simply isn't able to support you; you may need to look to other friends for that until she is feeling better. For your own self-preservation, too, reduce or limit the amount of time you spend together so you have the energy to listen without it sapping your energy. Another strategy would be to spend time with her in the company of other people.

Hope this helps.

Best,
Irene S Levine Ph.D.

Irene S. Levine, Ph.D., is a psychologist and professor of psychiatry at the NYU School of Medicine. Her latest book is Best Friends Forever: Surviving a Breakup With Your Best Friend.

DRAINS – HOW TO SPOT & NAVIGATE

"It's hard, when you're up to your armpits in alligators, to remember you came here to drain the swamp."
— *Ronald Reagan*

Identifying and Managing Emotionally Draining Individuals

In the complex world of interpersonal relationships, it's not uncommon to encounter individuals who leave you feeling utterly drained, like a sponge squeezed dry after a storm. These people, often labelled as "Drains," can have a significant impact on your mental and emotional well-being. This chapter explores how to recognise the signs of such individuals and provides strategies for navigating these challenging dynamics with skill and confidence.

Understanding Emotional Drain

Emotional drain, or emotional exhaustion, occurs when prolonged interactions with certain individuals consistently deplete your emotional resources. These people often exhibit specific traits and behaviours that can disturb your mental equilibrium, leading to heightened stress and reduced emotional resilience.

Key Traits of Emotionally Draining Individuals

1. **Constant Negativity**: These individuals maintain a persistently negative outlook, focusing on problems rather than solutions. Their relentless negativity can sap your optimism and energy.
2. **Excessive Drama**: Emotionally draining people tend to exaggerate minor issues, creating unnecessary drama that raises stress levels for those around them.

3. **Unresolved Emotional Baggage**: They carry unresolved emotional issues and often project these onto others, creating a repetitive cycle of negative interactions.

4. **Lack of Empathy**: Such individuals struggle to understand or connect with the emotions of others, leading to strained relationships and emotional fatigue.

5. **Manipulative Behaviour**: They may use guilt, coercion, or other manipulative tactics to control situations, leaving you feeling used and drained.

6. **Neediness and Dependency**: Emotionally draining people often require excessive attention and support, overwhelming those they interact with.

7. **Boundary Violations**: They frequently disregard personal boundaries, infringing on your space and autonomy, which can lead to emotional burnout.

The Impact of Emotional Drain

The effects of prolonged exposure to emotionally draining individuals can be profound. It can lead to emotional exhaustion, heightened stress, diminished self-esteem, and strained relationships. Over time, this can impede your personal and professional growth, making it crucial to recognise and address these dynamics early. In a perfect world, we would ignore these individuals, cast them onto an island where they cannot disrupt others perhaps? But in reality, they will already be embroiled in our life, our business and may even be our friends or relatives. So, these individuals need to be managed.

Strategies for Managing Emotionally Draining Individuals

1. **Establish Clear Boundaries**: Clearly define what behaviours are acceptable and what will not be tolerated. Communicate these boundaries in a firm way, avoiding conflict or anger, but making sure they are acknowledged and agreed upon. Remind them (the Drain) about your verbal agreement, and be consistent to safeguard your own well-being.

2. **Prioritise Self-Care**: Engage in activities that restore your energy and emotional balance. Regular exercise, mindfulness practices, and even a brisk walk in the fresh can help counterbalance the effects of emotional drain.

3. **Effective Communication**: Use assertive communication to address issues directly without escalating drama. This includes expressing your feelings calmly and setting clear expectations for future interactions.

4. **Limit Contact**: Where possible, reduce your exposure to emotionally draining individuals. This may involve limiting interactions or, in extreme cases, distancing yourself from the relationship.

5. **Seek Support**: Don't hesitate to seek support from friends, family, or professionals. Discussing your experiences with trusted individuals can provide new perspectives and coping strategies.

Self-Reflection: Identifying Your Own Behaviour

While it is essential to recognise emotionally draining behaviours in others, self-reflection is equally important. Assess whether you exhibit any of these traits in your interactions. Acknowledging and addressing these behaviours within yourself can lead to healthier relationships and improved emotional well-being.

By understanding the traits that characterise emotionally draining individuals and implementing strategies to manage these interactions, you can protect your emotional health. Remember, while you may not be able to change others, you can control how you respond to them. Prioritise your well-being through self-care, clear boundaries, and effective communication, ensuring that your energy remains intact even in the most challenging relationships

Navigating Constant Negativity: Strategies for Effective Leadership

Effective communication is a vital asset for leaders, particularly when dealing with the challenges of persistent negativity within a team or organisation. Leaders must be transparent in expressing their concerns and actively listen to others' perspectives. This open communication helps guide individuals towards greater self-awareness, enabling them to see how their negativity impacts both themselves and those around them.

Seeking support from mentors, peers, or professional advisors can be invaluable when managing ongoing negativity. These external voices offer insights, guidance, and emotional support, helping leaders navigate the complexities of emotionally draining interactions.

In some situations, it may be necessary to establish strategic distance and limit contact with those who are persistently negative. Prioritising your well-being and that of your team is crucial. Setting boundaries and reducing interaction can be a wise decision to maintain a healthy work environment.

Understanding the Dynamics of Excessive Drama

Excessive drama within a friendship group or a working team can sap energy and undermine productivity. Leaders should be aware of the following key traits associated with drama-driven behaviour:

Attention-Seeking: Individuals who thrive on drama often crave attention and may create or escalate conflicts to stay in the spotlight.

Lack of Self-Awareness: Those who engage in excessive drama may be unaware of the effects of their actions on others, perpetuating a cycle of conflict.

Repetitive Patterns: Drama-prone individuals tend to rehash old issues or initiate new conflicts, often without resolution.

Unrealistic Expectations: These individuals may demand constant validation and support, ignoring others' needs and boundaries.

Emotional Manipulation: Drama-driven individuals often know how to trigger negative emotions in others, creating a toxic atmosphere.

Energy Drain: Such behaviour depletes the emotional reserves of those involved, leaving team members feeling exhausted and demotivated.

Conflict Propensity: A tendency to seek or create conflict leads to a perpetual cycle of drama, hindering team cohesion.

Emotional Overload: These individuals often struggle to manage their emotions, offloading their turmoil onto others.

Imbalanced Relationships: Excessive drama creates an emotional imbalance in relationships, with one party consistently draining the energy of others.

To manage excessive drama effectively, leaders should set clear boundaries, prioritise self-care, and use effective communication strategies. Recognising when drama becomes overwhelming is essential, as is seeking support from others and potentially limiting contact with emotionally draining individuals.

Addressing Unresolved Emotional Baggage

Unresolved emotional baggage is often at the core of emotionally draining behaviour. This refers to past traumas or issues that remain unresolved, continuing to affect an individual and those around them, thereby straining relationships.

Repetitive Conflict: Individuals with unresolved baggage often revisit past issues, creating a negative environment that is exhausting for everyone involved.

Unrealistic Expectations and Lack of Awareness: These individuals may struggle to understand their emotions and their impact on others, often leading to unhealthy interactions.

Victim Mentality: A persistent sense of being wronged can lead to conflicts and hinder personal and professional growth.

Leaders should encourage those with unresolved emotional baggage to seek professional counselling. Additionally, setting clear boundaries is essential for protecting your own emotional well-being. Limiting contact may be necessary if their unresolved issues are negatively impacting team dynamics.

Managing a Lack of Empathy

Empathy is a cornerstone of effective leadership. When someone lacks empathy, it can strain relationships and disrupt team harmony. Leaders must be vigilant in identifying and addressing these challenges:

- Perspective Blindness: Those lacking empathy often dismiss others' feelings, undermining trust and collaboration.
- Self-Centredness: An inability to consider others' needs can lead to frustration and deteriorate team morale.
- Inadequate Emotional Support: Individuals who lack empathy may struggle to provide the necessary support during challenging times, leaving colleagues feeling isolated.
- Unintended Harm: Without empathy, individuals may inadvertently cause harm, leading to strained relationships and negative emotions.

To navigate these challenges, we should clearly communicate expectations, seek support from empathetic colleagues, and prioritise self-care. In cases where the lack of empathy becomes overwhelming, limiting interaction may be necessary to protect the group or team's emotional well-being.

Recognising and Addressing Manipulative Behaviour

Manipulative behaviour can be particularly challenging to manage within a team. Such behaviour often includes guilt-tripping, gaslighting, playing the victim, emotional blackmail, and manipulative language. We must be equipped with strategies to protect their groups or teams and maintain a positive environment.

Setting firm boundaries, practising self-care, and communicating effectively are essential. Additionally, seeking support from others and considering limited contact can help mitigate the negative impact of manipulative behaviour.

Handling Neediness and Dependency

Neediness and dependency can place undue strain on a team. Emotionally draining individuals may constantly seek validation and reassurance, leading to emotional exhaustion for those around them.

Validation Seeking: Constantly seeking approval can drain team resources and create an imbalance in relationships.

Emotional Reliance: Those who are overly dependent may struggle to manage their emotions independently, placing undue pressure on others.

We must set clear boundaries and communicate expectations effectively. Prioritising self-care is also essential to ensure that the emotional well-being of the team is maintained.

Overcoming Boundary Challenges

Individuals who struggle to establish boundaries can disrupt team dynamics and impact overall well-being. We need to be aware of the following challenges:

Overstepping Boundaries: Some individuals may invade personal space or make unwelcome demands, leading to discomfort and tension.

Ignoring Boundaries: Failing to respect others' boundaries can lead to feelings of disrespect and undervaluation.

Difficulty Saying No: A reluctance to say no can lead to exhaustion and resentment, especially when it goes against one's own needs.

Emotional Manipulation: Those who struggle with boundaries may resort to manipulation, creating a toxic environment.

Lack of Self-Awareness: Without awareness of their own emotions, these individuals perpetuate unhealthy dynamics.

Leaders should prioritise setting clear boundaries and communicating expectations effectively. Seeking support and practising self-care are essential for maintaining a healthy work environment.

The Impact of Emotionally Draining Individuals on a group's Well-being

Dealing with emotionally draining individuals can have significant consequences for a group or teams well-being. Special efforts are needed to be proactive in recognising and addressing these challenges:

Emotional Exhaustion: Constant exposure to negativity can lead to burnout and reduced productivity. Setting boundaries and seeking support are key to managing this impact.

Increased Stress: The constant demands and conflicts created by emotionally draining individuals can heighten stress levels. Leaders must prioritise self-care and consider distancing themselves from these individuals when necessary.

Reduced Self-Esteem: Persistent negativity and criticism can erode self-confidence. Leaders should focus on building a positive environment and seek support from trusted colleagues.

Strained Relationships: Constant conflict and manipulation can strain relationships within the team. Clear communication and boundary setting are crucial for maintaining harmony.

Hindered Personal Growth: Emotionally draining individuals can stifle personal and professional development. We must prioritise their own growth and set boundaries to protect their progress.

By recognising the signs of emotionally draining behaviour and taking proactive steps to address them, we can protect their well-being and foster a healthier, more productive work environment.

Reclaiming Your Energy: Navigating Emotional Demands for Personal Growth

Emotional demands and persistent negativity can drain your energy, shifting your focus from your own growth to the needs of others. This imbalance, if left unchecked, can stifle your personal and professional development. Yet, by taking decisive action, you can reclaim your energy and cultivate an environment that nurtures your own progress.

Setting Boundaries: Your Essential Defence

Establishing boundaries isn't just advisable—it's essential. Boundaries act as your armour, safeguarding your emotional well-being from those who sap your energy. Begin by clearly defining what is and isn't acceptable. Identify specific behaviours that leave you feeling depleted and communicate these limits with precision. Consistency is crucial; once established, ensure you uphold these boundaries firmly. This isn't about selfishness; it's about prioritising your mental health so that you have the resources to invest in your own growth.

Prioritising Self-Care: Reconnect and Recharge

Self-care is often neglected but is fundamental to maintaining mental and emotional health. Dedicate time to activities that rejuvenate you, whether through exercise, meditation, or indulging in a favourite hobby. These moments of self-reflection and relaxation are not luxuries—they are vital practices that help you recharge and remain grounded. They lay the foundation for your personal growth.

Communication: Mastering the Art of Managing Emotional Drains

Effective communication is key to handling relationships with emotionally draining individuals. Approach these interactions with assertiveness, clearly expressing your needs while remaining open to constructive dialogue. Use "I" statements to convey your feelings without assigning blame, and make sure to actively listen to the other person's perspective. This approach can often lead to solutions that benefit both parties, reducing the emotional burden these interactions may otherwise impose.

Seeking Support: You're Not Alone

Dealing with emotionally taxing relationships is challenging, but it's important to remember you don't have to do it on your own. Reach out to trusted friends, family, or professional advisors who can provide guidance and emotional support. Their perspectives can offer valuable insights, helping you navigate these situations more effectively. In some cases, seeking professional counselling may be necessary, particularly when dealing with deep-seated patterns of emotional drain.

Strategic Distance: The Power of Space

Sometimes, the most effective way to manage emotionally draining individuals is by limiting your exposure to them. This doesn't mean cutting ties completely, but rather being strategic about how and when you engage. Reducing contact can give you the space needed to focus on your own well-being and growth. It's about striking a balance that allows you to protect your mental health while maintaining important relationships.

Winning the Battle: Managing Emotional Turbulence

Dealing with emotionally draining people can feel like trying to win a dance-off against a tornado in a phone box—chaotic, exhausting, and seemingly impossible. But with the right strategies, you can navigate these challenges and emerge stronger. By setting boundaries, prioritising self-care, communicating effectively, seeking support, and strategically distancing yourself when necessary, you can reclaim your emotional energy and focus on what truly matters—your personal growth.

Conclusion: Reclaim Your Emotional Energy

Managing emotionally draining individuals is no small task, but it's vital for maintaining a balanced and healthy life. By setting boundaries, prioritising self-care, communicating effectively, seeking support, and sometimes creating distance, you can safeguard your emotional well-being and foster an environment where personal growth can thrive. Remember, you have the power to reclaim your emotional energy and channel it towards your own development and happiness.

Tips for Business and Life:

Navigating interactions with Drains is crucial for maintaining a balanced and healthy life. But we recognise that setting boundaries and prioritising self-care to safeguard your emotional well-being is easier said than done, so we've prepared some practical tips to help you reclaim your own emotional energy:

1. **Spot Drains from your own notes**

The first step in managing emotionally draining individuals is identifying behaviours that sap your energy. These may include constant negativity, excessive complaining, or manipulating emotions. Awareness is key to taking proactive steps to protect yourself.

Tip: Keep a private journal to track interactions and notice patterns that leave you feeling drained. Record date, time and names with key bullet points. This will help you identify who or what may be affecting your emotional energy.

2. Set Clear Boundaries

Establishing boundaries is essential for maintaining your emotional well-being. Be clear and assertive about your limits and communicate them calmly and respectfully with each Drain.

Tip: Practice saying "no" without guilt and set specific times for interactions that you find draining. Use phrases like "I need some time to recharge" or "Let me process our conversation" to communicate your needs.

3. Prioritise Self-Care

Self-care is not a luxury; it's a necessity. Dedicate time to activities that replenish your energy and bring you joy. This might include exercise, meditation, or spending time with loved ones.

Tip: Diarise regular self-care activities in your calendar just as you would any important meeting or appointment. Treat these times as non-negotiable and don't be derailed into giving them up.

4. Create a Supportive Network

This book will not only help you spot Drains but also Radiators. Surround yourself with positive, supportive individuals who uplift and inspire you. A strong support network can provide encouragement and help you navigate those challenging interactions.

Tip: Engage in communities or groups that share your interests and values. Attend events, workshops, or online forums to connect with like-minded people.

5. Focus on Personal Growth

Use your interactions with emotionally draining individuals as opportunities for personal growth. Reflect on what these experiences teach you about resilience, empathy, and strength.

Tip: After each draining interaction, take a moment to reflect on what you learned and how you can apply these insights to future situations. Consider journaling your reflections for deeper understanding.

6. Practice Mindfulness and Emotional Regulation

Develop mindfulness practices that help you stay grounded and calm during interactions with draining individuals. Techniques such as deep breathing, visualisation, or mindfulness meditation can help you manage your emotions effectively.

Tip: Before engaging with someone who drains your energy, take a few deep breaths and visualise yourself remaining calm and composed throughout the interaction.

By implementing these tips, you can effectively manage Drains, protect your emotional energy, and create a life where personal growth can flourish. Prioritising your well-being is vital for building resilience and fostering an environment that nurtures both your personal and professional development.

IV

RADIATORS – HOW TO FIND & KEEP IN YOUR ORBIT

'Keep your face always toward the sunshine - and shadows will fall behind you.' Walt Whitman

Surrounding Yourself with the Right People Changes Everything

It's well-known that one of the best ways to improve any skill is to practise it with someone who's better than you (think: golf, tennis, skiing, yoga, chess—the list goes on). Yes, you'll need to work harder, think faster, and master the basics, but that's what drives us to push beyond our limits. You might sweat and ache, but over time, your skills will sharpen, and before long, you could find yourself in a position to teach others. This idea of "playing with someone better" also applies to our personal and professional lives, which is why it's crucial to surround yourself with people who are winners.

Many of the world's top thought leaders, entrepreneurs, and entertainers—including motivational coach Tony Robbins, British entrepreneur and Dragon Steven Bartlett, Cirque du Soleil founder Guy Laliberté, and #MeToo pioneer Tarana Burke—agree that success often hinges on who's got your back. It's hard not to be inspired by these remarkable individuals. Their stories and life lessons can fill us with new ideas and energy.

Here are some practical steps to help you apply this concept to your own life.

Say Goodbye to Toxic Colleagues and Negative Nellies

We all recognise those colleagues or acquaintances who are constantly embroiled in turmoil or drama, and who never seem to rise above their victim status. Worse still, they try to drag you down with them.

Life is challenging enough as it is—we don't always win, and obstacles and naysayers will always be part of the journey. In such times, nothing feels better than having someone you can share your fears and doubts with—friends and mentors who not only listen but also cheer you on to be the best you can be. "Get back in there and do better! You can do it!" These are the people who energise you and help you propel forward.

Focus on building relationships with those who share their wins and positive vibes, and help you realise that you can do the same. Life is too short to be weighed down by constant negativity.

Find People Who Are Smarter Than You

Many entrepreneurs and businesspeople aspire to be the smartest person in the room, but if you're always the smartest, you're actually limiting yourself. Jim Rohn famously said, "You're the average of the five people you spend the most time with." It's easy to underestimate the importance of the company we keep. We need people—whether they're teachers, mentors, family, or trusted friends—who challenge us and push us to be better. The right circle of influence raises the bar, helping us set new, higher expectations for ourselves.

Often, we don't realise what we're capable of until we see others achieve. It's no coincidence that, according to Glassdoor's Best Places to Work 2024 in the UK, organisations like Bain & Company, Mastercard, and Boston Consulting Group are so popular and successful among high achievers.

When we surround ourselves with positive, successful people, they consciously (and subconsciously) challenge us to be our best selves.

Cultivate "Real Life" Relationships with People Who Have Already Achieved Your Goals

It's time to rethink how we use social media and focus on our "real life" relationships. Today's social media feeds can often be a reminder of what we can't do, haven't done, or don't believe we can accomplish. Seeing someone's online "highlight reel" doesn't truly show you what goes on behind the scenes and how much work it really requires. Spend time focusing on the process of success, not just the results.

Highly successful people are usually willing to share what it really takes to make things happen. They can help you learn from their mistakes and share tips and tricks to help you reach your goals faster. Seek out leaders in your field and get some real face time with them.

If You Can't Play Golf, Watch the Game

American author, business consultant, and motivational speaker Ken Blanchard has written over 60 books, my favourite being The One Minute Manager. He once said, "None of us is as smart as all of us." That perfectly sums up why we should learn from others.

Observing, copying, and adapting from books, blogs, videos, and lectures all help prepare us to do things differently. There's a poem that beautifully illustrates the importance of learning from others: "The Blind Men and the Elephant" by John Godfrey Saxe.

It's a famous Indian fable about six blind men who each encounter different parts of an elephant. Each man then constructs his own version of reality based on his limited perspective and experience:

It was six men of Indostan,
To learning much inclined,
Who went to see the Elephant
(Though all of them were blind),
That each by observation
Might satisfy his mind.
The First approached the Elephant,
And happening to fall
Against his broad and sturdy side,
At once began to bawl:
"God bless me! but the Elephant
Is very like a wall!"
The Second, feeling of the tusk,

Cried, "Ho! what have we here
So very round and smooth and sharp?
To me 'tis mighty clear,
This wonder of an Elephant
Is very like a spear!"
The Third approached the animal,
And happening to take
The squirming trunk within his hands,
Thus boldly up and spake:
"I see," -quoth he- "the Elephant
Is very like a snake!"
The Fourth reached out an eager hand,
And felt about the knee:
"What most this wondrous beast is like
Is mighty plain," -quoth he,-
"'Tis clear enough the Elephant
Is very like a tree!"
The Fifth, who chanced to touch the ear,
Said- "E'en the blindest man
Can tell what this resembles most;
Deny the fact who can,
This marvel of an Elephant
Is very like a fan!"
The Sixth no sooner had begun
About the beast to grope,
Then, seizing on the swinging tail
That fell within his scope,
"I see," -quoth he,- "the Elephant
Is very like a rope!"
And so these men of Indostan
Disputed loud and long,

Each in his own opinion
Exceeding stiff and strong,
Though each was partly in the right,
And all were in the wrong!

The Main Lesson from the Poem:

Our limited perspectives and experiences can mistakenly cause us to believe our view is the only reality. This is one of the pitfalls of solo learning and failing to consider others' perspectives.

Why We Need to Learn from Others

Once we accept that we can't know everything, we can embrace the concept of learning from others and practising reflective listening. While there are countless strategies to learn independently, and many guides for self-invention and solo entrepreneurship, these often overlook the crucial role that others play in our learning and success. The people we interact with are integral to our eventual achievements or failures.

A Few of the Benefits of Learning from Others

When we learn from others, we gain several benefits that can't be achieved alone, including:

1. Leveraging Prosocial Motivation:

Learning from others can spark a unique form of motivation known as "prosocial motivation," which is simply the desire to assist and encourage others. Think of it as a quality for life.

The main advantage of prosocial motivation is that when we hit roadblocks and doubt our ability to continue, the relationships around us provide strength and support. This type of motivation is crucial in the learning journey.

2. They Know and See Things We Don't—Gaining Different Perspectives:

It might seem obvious, but many of us focus solely on what we know and see, forgetting to explore alternative perspectives. Working with others who know things you don't gives you access to new knowledge and, even if you don't agree or like the alternative, it can lead to a refreshing compromise.

A real-life example is Apple's famous business comeback. In 1997, they were struggling after 12 consecutive years of financial losses. In a desperate move, Apple's board of directors ousted CEO Gil Amelio and brought back co-founder Steve Jobs to try to revive the company.

One of Jobs' first acts was to announce a five-year partnership with rival Microsoft, initially met with rejection and dismay. It was a rare moment of humility for Jobs, who said, "We have to let go of this notion that for Apple to win, Microsoft has to lose."

What followed was one of the most impressive runs of innovation in consumer product history, and the world is a different place today thanks to the iPhone, iPad, iMac, and other Apple inventions. Without that fresh perspective, Apple could have been a distant memory.

3. We Process Information Better:

When we work with others, we can combine our knowledge to solve problems differently. This allows us to process information in new ways and use novel approaches to problem-solving. A common technique here is group brainstorming.

Effective brainstorming sessions include:

Rapid ideation: In a short timeframe, like two minutes, all members write down as many ideas as they can for solving the problem. The limited time encourages pure and genuine expression.

Stepladder technique: Introduce the topic, and allow two people to brainstorm together. Then, add a third person to share their ideas, and a fourth, and so on. This method allows team members to build on one another's insights.

Mind mapping: Ideas branch off one another, creating a web of possible solutions. Visual representation can help teams develop a solution that works for everyone.

New location: Try brainstorming in different environments, like outdoors. A change of scenery can help stimulate creativity.

Figure storming: Choose a figure, like a company owner, manager, celebrity, or fictional character, and discuss how that person might solve the problem. This approach encourages team members to think beyond their perspectives.

Mood board: A collection of words and images related to one central idea. This tool can help organise thoughts and keep the team focused on the topic.

Group sketching: Each group member takes turns drawing a potential solution, then passes the sketch to the next person, who adds their features. Each idea builds upon the last until you have a collection of visual representations.

If you want to become your best self, I challenge you to review, rethink, and curate your social media, business contacts, and real-life "friends" to find the right people and media content that will actually help you get there. Ignore the noise and clutter that holds you back.

How to Keep Radiators in Your Orbit

What's the secret to retaining your best people? We take a lesson from Emily Frieze-Kemeny, CEO and Founder of AROSE Group, a leadership consulting firm that blends humanity with profitability. Emily shares three startling facts:

1. We Should Fear Losing Top Talent: It's natural to worry about losing your best performers, and rightly so. Exceptional leaders and high achievers significantly drive an organisation's success.

2. People Are The Turnover Threat: According to CNBC, over 60% of employees are considering leaving their jobs at any moment, with the numbers even higher among Gen Z and millennials and people contribute to loss of turnover more than anything else.

3. Instability Concerns: With ongoing downsizings and restructurings, job security fears are on the rise, leading to an increased likelihood of your top people taking that call from a recruiter or competitor.

But before we throw in the towel, complain about the younger workforce, or start dishing out retention bonuses, let's take a moment for some introspection.

The AROSE Group developed the "Four Ps to Retention" framework, which offers a strategic approach to keeping your best people engaged and committed. Here's how you can apply these four key principles—Probative, Prerogative, Purposeful, and Proactive—to your own retention strategy.

Probative: Dig Deep to Understand Why People Leave

Exit interviews alone won't cut it. By the time someone is walking out the door, it's often too late to get the full picture. People might say they're leaving for career growth, new opportunities, or family reasons, but these are often just surface explanations. The real reasons often lie deeper, such as:

- Work overload
- Lack of resources or funding
- Inability to collaborate across departments
- Issues with management or colleagues
- Cultural misfit
- Not feeling valued

Turnover is easy to track, and the numbers speak for themselves. If retention is an issue in your organisation, try conducting one-to-one stay interviews or focus groups with those who may be considering a change. During regular check-ins, managers should probe to understand what's working for their team members and what changes could help them reach their full potential.

Sometimes, the manager might be the problem. To address this, consider having senior leaders conduct informal skip-level one-to-ones with team members to gain unfiltered insights.

Prerogative: Understand Who Your Organisation Truly Needs

Retention isn't always the goal. Sometimes, it's best for both the employee and the organisation to part ways. Reasons for this might include:

Misalignment with Business Needs: The work an employee wants to do no longer aligns with the organisation's goals. In such cases, it's crucial to treat them well and ensure they become external advocates for your organisation.

Toxic Attitude: If someone's attitude has soured due to perceived stagnation or frustration, it can spread negativity throughout the team. Holding on to toxic employees can endanger the morale of your best people, so it's important to act decisively.

Poor Cultural or Leadership Fit: Perhaps the employee was never the right fit, or changes in leadership have created friction. Misalignment in culture or leadership styles is a significant driver of attrition, so it's vital to assess and address these issues promptly.

Purposeful: Win Back the Hearts and Minds of Those on the Fence

High performers who work well with others and drive great results are worth their weight in gold. However, they're also the hardest to retain. Their passion for excellence can make them intolerant of stagnation or underperforming colleagues, and they are often sought after by other organisations. To retain them, you need to be hyper-aware of their needs and motivations.

How can you stay vigilant? By truly getting to know your top performers—what drives them, what frustrates them, and what excites them. Managers and mentors should invest time in listening to their concerns and aspirations. Regularly remind them of their value to the organisation and provide clear pathways for their career growth. You can never over-communicate this.

Proactive: Stay Ahead of Retention Risks

A successful retention strategy isn't just about equipping managers; it requires strong organisational design, a commitment to continuous improvement, and personalised incentives.

Role Crafting: Sometimes, you need to shape a role around your best people rather than forcing them into a predefined box. Create roles that maximise their strengths and keep them engaged.

Team Crafting: Build teams that energise your top performers. Working alongside talented and collaborative colleagues can be incredibly motivating and helps retain your best talent.

Customised Rewards: Let employees choose their rewards from a range of options, such as cash bonuses, childcare support, professional development funds, coaching, wellness services, additional time off, or flexible work schedules.

New Opportunities: Offer your top people the chance to work on exciting projects, engage in strategic learning experiences, and gain exposure to senior leaders and key clients. This keeps them engaged and invested in your organisation.

Promote Before They Ask: Don't wait for your high performers to seek recognition. Offer promotions and pay raises before they feel the need to ask.

By creating an environment that attracts and retains top talent, you'll see your organisation thrive. When you actively ask, listen, learn, and align your people with the right roles, teams, rewards, and challenges, everyone benefits—and your results will speak for themselves.

The Richer Way – key lessons for retaining radiators and ditching the drains

The first business book we ever read from cover to cover was The Richer Way by Julian Richer. It was impossible to put down because, unlike many businesses management books, it didn't revel in theories and business philosophy, but provided a firsthand practical guide on how to get the best out of people.

In case you don't know who Julian Richer is, in 1978 aged just nineteen, he opened his first shop near London Bridge. For over twenty years this shop was listed in the Guinness Book of Records as having the highest sales per square foot of any retail outlet in the world, and the company as a whole, with its fifty-three stores nationwide and huge online presence, has become Britain's favourite retailer of TV and hi-fi equipment. So what lies behind this extraordinary success?

For Julian, the answer was simple: throughout his career he has focussed relentlessly on putting people - both staff and customers - right at the centre of his business. And in The Richer Way, he offers a supremely practical guide to how others can follow suit. He explains how to motivate employees and measure their progress. He establishes how to balance company discipline with individual autonomy. He explores what 'customer service' should really involve. Above all, he points the way to creating an open, friendly and flexible culture that will not only attract the best people but also offer the greatest chance of business success.

Having re-read Julians book (I still have it in a box under the stairs), I can summarise the key learnings as follows:

1. **Adopt People-Centric Leadership:**

Julian Richer emphasises that employees are the most valuable asset of any business. Treating them well, investing in their development, and fostering a positive work environment leads to higher motivation, loyalty, and productivity. Key strategies include:

Fairness and Respect: Ensure that all employees are treated with respect and fairness, regardless of their role.

Engagement: Regularly involve staff in decision-making and encourage their input on business matters.

Recognition: Celebrate achievements and recognise hard work to boost morale and motivation.

2. **Follow Ethical Business Practices:**

Richer advocates for maintaining high ethical standards in all business dealings. This includes:

Honesty: Be transparent with customers, employees, and suppliers. Trust is a cornerstone of long-term success.

Social Responsibility: Run a business that contributes positively to society, whether through charitable activities or by operating sustainably.

Fair Trading: Engage in fair competition and ensure that your business practices are not only legally compliant but morally sound.

3. **Focus on the Long Term:**

The book stresses the importance of thinking beyond short-term gains. Successful businesses build lasting relationships with customers and employees by:

Customer Care: Provide exceptional service and aftercare, ensuring customers feel valued and supported.

Quality Over Quantity: Focus on delivering high-quality products and services rather than cutting corners to save costs.

Sustainable Growth: Avoid the temptation of rapid expansion that could jeopardise the company's core values or stability.

4. **Strive For Continuous Improvement:**

Richer underscores the need for constant evolution and adaptation in business. Key practices include:

Training and Development: Regularly upskill employees to keep them motivated and prepared for industry changes.

Feedback Loops: Encourage feedback from both customers and employees to identify areas for improvement.

Innovation: Stay ahead by embracing new technologies and ideas that can enhance the business.

5. **Financial Prudence Rules:**

Managing finances wisely is crucial. Richer advises:

Cost Control: Keep a close eye on expenses without compromising quality.

Cash Flow Management: Ensure the business always has sufficient cash reserves to handle unexpected challenges.

Investment in the Future: Reinvest profits into the business for growth and improvement rather than prioritising immediate personal gains.

6. **Lead by Example:**

As a leader, embody the values and principles you want your company to reflect. This includes:

Humility: Stay grounded, regardless of the company's success.

Integrity: Uphold high moral standards in all actions and decisions.

Empathy: Understand and consider the perspectives of others in your leadership approach.

By applying these principles from 'The Richer Way,' businesses can build a solid foundation for sustained success, employee satisfaction, and ethical growth.

Julian has gone on to chalk up some notable achievements in business over the last 50 years – including setting up Richer Sounds, in his capacity as a business advisor to Asda and to M&S, and in his extensive not-for-profit work – is a belief that business is all about people.

Julian believes you observe a different output depending on how you treat people. By making work fun, providing more recognition, communicating clearly, rewarding achievements and by being loyal to your colleagues, you'll see a very real payback in terms of your operational success and profitability.

But Julian advocates a step further in his teachings, laying out a clear challenge that we must get better at differentiating between 'good' and 'bad' capitalism.

He says that capitalism, as we've seen throughout history, has the power to drive innovation but has also been a source of suffering and exploitation. Concerns around fairness, zero-hours contracts and the tax gap are some examples of persistent issues. This has driven Julian to set up several nonprofits to address these issues since handing over his Richer Sounds business to an employee-owned trust in 2019.

For Julian, outside of any altruistic motivations, this differentiation requires a mindset shift to see the long-term opportunity cost of ethical capitalism. Doing 'the right thing' might in the short term be less profitable, but the benefits organisations will see in productivity and retention in the longer term are invaluable.

From a consumer point of view, leading on ethical capitalism could have huge benefits, with 97% of the public indicating they want to spend their money in a socially conscious way. Julian set up the Good Business Charter, which the Forward Institute has signed up to, to provide consumers with a choice of who they do business with.

At the Forward Institute, being brave is a core principle of our thinking on responsible leadership. Change comes about when leaders feel they have legitimacy to act on an issue. It's our role to advocate, inspire and fight against the short-termism that so often lends itself to self-interest.

Julian left us with the provocation that when it comes to ethical capitalism, the best place for each of us to begin is often just to "start doing something" that can take hold – brainstorm ideas with colleagues and reposition your organisation for the long-term gain.

Tips for Business and Life:

We've discovered in this chapter that people can determine your success in business and in life, so to help you keep radiators close and loyal to you, here are some tips that will hold true:

1. **Seek Smarter Company:** Steer clear of colleagues who thrive on negativity and drama but don't aim to be the smartest in the room. Surround yourself with people who challenge you, raise your standards, and inspire you to achieve more.

2. **Focus on Real Relationships and Learn from Others:** Build meaningful, real-life connections with successful individuals who can offer genuine insights and guidance. Learn from their experiences to fast-track your own success. Embrace the wisdom and experience of others. Collaboration and learning from those who've already succeeded can help you grow and achieve your goals more effectively.

3. **Prioritise People-Centric Leadership:** Treat Employees as Assets: Your staff are the backbone of your business. Invest in their growth, treat them with respect, and they will drive your success. Foster Engagement by involving your team in

decision-making processes. Listen to their ideas and concerns to build a more inclusive and motivated workforce.

4. **Uphold Ethical Business Practices:** Be Transparent: Honesty with customers, employees, and partners is key to building trust and long-term relationships. Practice Social Responsibility: Contribute positively to society through sustainable practices and community involvement. Ensure Fair Trading: Engage in ethical business practices, competing fairly and treating all stakeholders with integrity.

5. **Focus on Long-Term Success:** Deliver Quality: Prioritise high-quality products and services over quick profits. Quality builds customer loyalty. Provide Exceptional Service: Go the extra mile in customer service to ensure satisfaction and repeat business. Sustain Growth: Avoid the pitfalls of rapid expansion. Build your business steadily, preserving core values.

6. **Embrace Continuous Improvement:** Invest in Development: Regularly upskill your team to keep them engaged and ahead of industry trends. Encourage Feedback: Create open channels for feedback from both employees and customers. Use it to improve continuously. Innovate Constantly: Stay competitive by adopting new technologies and creative solutions that enhance your business.

7. **Exercise Financial Prudence:** Control Costs: Monitor expenses closely without sacrificing quality. Efficient spending strengthens your financial

foundation. Manage Cash Flow: Ensure you have adequate cash reserves to handle unexpected challenges and opportunities. Reinvest in Growth: Reinvest profits into your business for future growth rather than focusing on short-term gains.

8. **Lead by Example: Show Humility:** Stay grounded and approachable, regardless of your business's success. Act with Integrity: Uphold high ethical standards in all your decisions and actions. Practice Empathy: Understand and consider the perspectives of others, fostering a more compassionate and effective leadership style.

By adopting these principles, you can cultivate a thriving business culture that not only retains talent, especially the radiators, but also contributes positively to society, ensuring long-term success and ethical growth.

V CAN DRAINS BECOME RADIATORS?

'Every person gets negative things, they learn from those negative things, and you become a positive person' Kapil Dev

Turning Negatives into Positives

We all start life as drains, so we know what negativity feels like. We've all had our dark moments, but for those we consider as pure drains, the constant battle to keep negativity at bay can be exhausting. They may even envy those who seem to navigate life with ease.

However, the inner voice that influences our reactions and behaviour is entirely natural, whether you're a radiator or a drain. The difference lies in how well we manage it. So, can drains become radiators? The answer is yes, but it requires the right skills and processes.

Quieten the Negative Inner Voice

When our brain senses danger, it releases stress hormones like adrenaline and cortisol to protect us. While this response was essential when we were outrunning predators, too much of these chemicals can make us ill in today's world.

That inner voice can sometimes motivate us, but it also says things like, "I could never do that," or "They all hate me." Managing this voice is key to turning negatives into positives.

Coping Under Pressure

I remember my first large-scale work project—an overwhelming task for a global hotel brand that involved creating a bespoke welcome guide for each of their locations. It was my first major agency job, and I was out of my comfort zone, plagued by thoughts like, "I'm really messing this up."

These doubts almost became a self-fulfilling prophecy, sapping my confidence and turning me into what I believed to be a burden to others. I felt like a fraud, relying too much on others, even as junior staff started showing me how to do things. I was convinced I was becoming a drain, and everyone saw me as an impostor.

These feelings lasted until the project's deadline. On the final day, my boss called me into his office. Expecting a dressing down, I prepared for the worst. Instead, he praised my performance, apologised for not offering more support, and expressed excitement about working with me again. My internal negativity was miles apart from how I actually performed. I felt like a drain but had behaved like a radiator.

Are Negative Thoughts Taking Over Your Life?

Negative thoughts might come and go or linger more persistently. When they spiral out of control, they can ruin not just your day but your life. They can hold you back from pursuing promotions, jobs, relationships, and opportunities, stunting your growth and leading you down a path of poor decisions and self-doubt. These thoughts can warp your perception of reality and even cause physical and mental health issues.

One common metaphor for this is the "monkey on your back," a burden or problem that's hard to shake off. This persistent negativity can feel like an unyielding weight, dragging you down with every step.

Understanding Your Inner Chimp

We've all experienced feelings of boredom, loneliness, and lethargy. The pandemic exacerbated these emotions, increasing stress, anxiety, and negative thought patterns. Professor Steve Peters, who introduced the "Chimp" concept, explains that this primal part of our brain stores emotional memories and tries to protect us from emotional pain. However, it often does so by flooding our minds with negative thoughts and anxieties.

This "Chimp" is quick to hit the panic button, reacting before our logical mind can take over. It's why we might overreact to minor setbacks or spend an entire day worrying about things that may never happen.

Negative Thoughts Can Take Many Forms

The thing about negative thoughts is that they don't usually reflect reality. In the 1960s, U.S. psychiatrist Aaron Beck recognised specific patterns to negative thinking, which he called "Cognitive Distortions" or "Distorted Thinking."

They're common, entirely normal, and not our fault. Beck's pioneering research formed a central part of his cognitive theory of depression and, later, Cognitive Behavioural Therapy (CBT).

Since then, researchers have developed his ideas and identified 10 common distorted thinking patterns as follows:

1. Polarised Thinking

Example: You're in high school and your thoughts are "If I don't get straight As, I've essentially failed."

2. Overgeneralisation

Example: When you break up with someone and tell yourself "This always happens, I'll never find anyone," or when you burn the toast and think, "Why does nothing ever go right for me?"

3. Mental Filtering

Example: You're starting out in your career and all you can think about is getting the promotion, why haven't you made it yet, will someone get there before you, you're thoughts are "Without the next promotion, I'm such a failure"

You've filtered out the fact that you'd managed to land such a great job, had wonderful clients, great friends, and a supportive partner and to others, you were the picture of success.

4. Discounting the Positive

Example: You find yourself in a slump, and catch yourself saying "Sure, I might be a decent copywriter, but anybody can learn how to do that."

5. Mindreading

Example: Your partner introduces me to their friends and you spend the entire journey home thinking, "They all hate me, I told that stupid story and now they all think I'm boring."

A couple of hours later you peak at the group chat, where everyone had been singing your praises.

6. Catastrophising

Example: The time a client hired a full-time writer, and I lost their business and automatically assumed, "I'm going to lose all my other clients, then I'll have to move out and live in my parents' shed."

7. Emotional Reasoning

Example: You apply for a job that seems perfect but think "I'm so worthless, there's no point in even trying – I'd never get the job anyway." Spoiler: You get the job.

8. "Should" Statements

Example: When you're rigid with ideas about how you should or shouldn't be spending your free time, "I should be getting up early and start every morning with yoga." You then feel anxious and blame yourself when you are too tired to manage it.

9. Labelling

Example: The time you assumed that your ex-colleague was a horrible person because she was a bit "short" with you when you first met. Spoiler: She was just having a nightmare Monday, and you became really good friends.

10. Personalisation and Blame

Example: When your ex-boss used to look annoyed and you would instantly shrink into yourself and think, "I must have done something wrong, I can't do anything right."

Tips for Turning Negative Thoughts into Positive Actions

Having continuous negative thoughts, or being a constant drain, is like being a drug addict. Due to the process of neuroplasticity, habitual negative thinking patterns wear such a path that they become physical neural traits in your brain. Scientists say that our brains are always looking to make habits because they're always looking for ways to save effort.

But a habit cannot be eradicated; only replaced. Just like the drug addiction, you need to replace the bad drug with something less harmful. With negativity, you have to go back to the very beginning of the stimulus/response cycle and replace the current response with a different one.

How many times have you listed all the positive steps you're going to take, then not acted on them? That's because the longer you think about doing something, the less likely you are to do it. Negative thoughts will talk you out of it.

Don't make negative thinking a lifelong habit. Here are some tips for getting your brain and mind to work with you. Your actions will prompt more positive thinking too!

1. Start a Journal: Track your thoughts daily to identify triggers and patterns. This helps in addressing negative thoughts before they spiral out of control.
2. Ask Yourself, "What Would I Say to a Friend?": We tend to be kinder to others than to ourselves. Reframe your negative thoughts by considering how you would advise a friend in a similar situation.
3. Say "Stop": When you catch your inner Chimp acting up, say "Stop" out loud and redirect your thoughts.
4. Change Negativity to Neutrality: Instead of forcing yourself to be positive, aim to be neutral. For example, change, "This is impossible," to "Let's try a different approach."
5. Create an SOS File of Positive Praise: Keep a collection of positive feedback and compliments to remind yourself of your achievements when you're

feeling low. An affirmation journal can be used to top up your self-esteem bucket when you need it most.

6. Breathe: Practise deep breathing exercises to calm your mind and body, making it easier to think clearly.

7. Talk to Somebody: Share your thoughts with a trusted friend, colleague, or therapist who can help you gain perspective.

8. Follow a Healthy Lifestyle: Regular exercise, a balanced diet, and getting outside can significantly improve your mood and energy levels.

9. Identify Areas to Change: Focus on one area of your life that you often think negatively about and work on changing your mindset there.

10. Surround Yourself With Positive People: Seek out supportive individuals who encourage you and help you manage your negative thoughts.

11. Practice Self-Compassion: Be gentle with yourself. Recognise that everyone has flaws, and that self-criticism only keeps you stuck.

12. Practice Positive Self-Talk Out Loud: Use your name instead of "I" to create emotional distance and think more rationally about your situation.

This is the positive impact of change. By changing how you think and act, you can physically rewire your brain, leading to more realistic and positive thinking over time. With consistent effort, you'll notice an increase in confidence, achievements, and opportunities.

A Good Boss These Days Is Hard To Find...

This might sound like a poor copy of Feargal Sharkey's classic hit, but it is a truism. A good boss will devote time to personal development, nurture their people and make them better at their job. But as businesses grow and departments evolve, the hands-on boss is typically superseded by HR staff who manage performance, training and promotions based on objectives and targets. Those that meet the needs of the job excel, those that don't get stuck or worse still, managed out.

But what can business owners do to get more from their teams and ultimately swop out those drain-like behaviours to more radiator-like qualities?

7 Things Business Leaders Do to Help People Change

Change is hard. Whether it's getting your colleagues to adopt a new system, or convincing your team to work differently, trying to influence people can be a frustrating, thankless task. But some business leaders seem to do it better than others. So, what's their secret?

In a study conducted by Harvard Business Publishing, researchers looked at 2,852 direct reports of 559 leaders, rating their managers on 49 behaviours and assessing their effectiveness at leading change. They found seven key behaviours that really help people to change.

But before we share these 7 tips, let us quash the myth that *'being nice'* to others is the best way to prompt change, in fact being the nice guys finished last in the change game. It might be easier if all it took to bring about change was to have a warm, positive relationship with others. But that isn't the case.

Giving in to others incessant requests, suggestions, and advice actually serves to make drains, well, even more drain-like. Thankfully, the team at Harvard analysed the behaviours that did correlate with an exceptional ability to drive change and they found that these seven really help other people to change. Here they are, in order from most to least important:

1. **Inspiring others.** There are two common approaches that most of us default to when trying to motivate others to change. Broadly, we could label them "Push" and "Pull." Some people intuitively push others, forcefully telling them they need to change, providing frequent reminders and sometimes following these steps with a warning about consequences if they don't change. This is the classic "hand in your back" approach to motivating change. (We noted earlier that classic "Push" doesn't work well.)

   The alternative approach is "Pull," which we can employ in a variety of ways. These include working with the individual to set an aspirational goal, exploring alternative avenues to reach an objective, and seeking other's ideas for the best methods to use going forward. This approach works best when you begin by identifying what the other person wants to achieve and making the link between that goal and the change you're proposing. Inspiring leaders understand the need for making an emotional connection with colleagues. They want to provoke a sense of desire rather than fear. Another approach in many work situations is to make a compelling, rational connection with the individual in which we explain the logic for the change we want them to make.

2. **Noticing problems.** Lots of management advice focuses on the need for individuals to become better problem solvers; but there is an important step that comes even earlier. It is the ability to recognise problems (to see situations where change is needed and to anticipate potential snares in advance).

   For example, in one company they worked with, it was common to hear people being praised for their heroic crisis management skills – rescuing projects on the brink of failure or getting a delayed product to a client just in time. A new manager recognised this pattern as a serious problem. She correctly saw it not as a sign of hard work, but as a symptom of a broken process.

3. **Providing a clear goal.** The farmer attempting to plow straight furrows selects a point in the distance and then constantly aims in that direction. Change initiatives work best when everyone's sight is fixed

on the same goal. Therefore, the most productive discussions about any change being proposed are those that start with the strategy that it serves.

4. **Challenging standard approaches.** Successful change efforts often require leaders to challenge standard approaches and find ways to maneuver around old practices and policies – even sacred cows. Leaders who excel at driving change will challenge even the rules that seem carved in stone.

5. **Building trust in your judgment.** This is both about actually improving your judgment and improving others' perceptions of it. Good leaders make decisions carefully after collecting data from multiple sources and seeking opinions from those whom they know will have differing views. They recognise that asking others for advice is evidence of their confidence and strength, not a sign of weakness. Because of their ability to build trust in the decisions they make, their ability to change the organization skyrockets. If others do not trust your judgment, it will be difficult to get them to make the changes you want them to make.

6. **Having courage.** Aristotle said, "You will never do anything in this world without courage. It is the greatest quality of the mind next to honour." Indeed, every initiative you begin as a leader, every new hire you make, every change in process you implement, every new product idea you pursue, every reorganisation you implement, every speech

you deliver, every conversation in which you give difficult feedback to a colleague, and every investment in a new piece of equipment requires courage. The need for courage covers many realms.

We sometimes hear people say, "Oh, I'm not comfortable doing that." Our observation is that a great deal of what leaders do, and especially their change efforts, demands willingness to live in discomfort.

7. **Making change a top priority.** One of Newton's Laws of Thermodynamics was that a body at rest tends to stay at rest. Slowing down, stopping, and staying at rest does not require effort. It happens very naturally. Many change efforts are not successful because they become one of a hundred priorities. To make a change effort successful you need to clear away the competing priorities and shine a spotlight on this one change effort. Leaders who do this well have a daily focus on the change effort, track its progress carefully and encourage others.

Becoming a change enabler will benefit every aspect of your life, both at home and in business. It will even help you to change yourself.

Tips for Business and Life:

It's not easy being a modern business leader who strives to help people become more positive and less needy and so here are some helpful tips based on the content in this this chapter that will help:

1. **Praise and celebrate:** Recognise and celebrate the accomplishments of your team members or your circle of friends and reward them accordingly. This will create a positive impact on their mood, boost their morale and strengthen any bonds you have. Remember that rewards don't have to be financial, a thoughtful card or handwritten note goes a long way.

2. **Encourage independence:** Give your team members the freedom to work independently and allow them to take ownership of their work. Help friends and family on their path to independence by giving them introductions and recommendations that improve their connections.

3. **Provide support:** Provide a forum for two-way dialogue and encourage your team to talk openly about their challenges. Provide support and guidance to friends and family wherever possible.

4. **Set realistic goals:** Set realistic goals for yourself and your team members and work together to achieve them over time. With friends and family, the same process applies for ambitions and life goals.

5. **Promote positivity:** Encourage positivity by fostering an environment of open communication, where everyone can express their thoughts and feelings. This can be ad-hoc and opportunistic or diarised as a catch-up with purpose.

6. **Encourage healthy habits:** Encourage your team, friends and family members to take care of their physical and mental health, by providing them access to resources that help them stay healthy both on and off the job.

7. **Be approachable:** Whilst open-door policy is sometimes hard to maintain, adopting an approachable demeaner that fosters open communication and honesty works in business and private in equal measure.

8. **Build trust:** Trust is a two-way thing but we can establish a foundation of trust by being honest, transparent, and consistent in our actions, behaviour and communication.

9. **Lead by example:** Being a modern business leader means setting an example for how others should behave. Lead by your own example and encourage your team to follow. Adopt this approach for your own circle of friends by demonstrating your own virtues of stability in family life.

10. **Prioritise balance:** Many of us struggle with work-life balance but by encouraging your team to maintain a healthy balance between their professional and personal life by taking breaks and engaging in activities outside of work demonstrates understanding and apathy.

These tips serve to help us all to become less drain-like in our approach to work and life. The constant battle to keep negativity at bay can be softened by a good boss or simply someone to look up to. Creating a more positive you and being more supportive in work and in friendships is rewarding in itself, it promotes positivity, productivity, and personal growth without feeling like hard work, and that's half the battle won.

VI CAN RADIATORS BECOME DRAINS?

"Absolute power corrupts absolutely" John Emerich Edward Dalberg Acton, first Baron Acton (1834–1902)

From the next Steve Jobs to drain-like villain?

We thought long and hard about this chapter; how can we best share our understanding of how people can go from being a positive radiator to a negative drain. Rather than provide an opposite perspective of the previous chapter we thought it best to illustrate the perils of becoming a drain with a real-life story.

There are many disgraced leaders that we could reference here but the story of former Theranos CEO Elizabeth Holmes is one that shows how a truly inspirational leader, someone with genuine radiator qualities became the ultimate drain.

More than three years after Elizabeth Holmes was first indicted and nearly four months after her trial kicked off, the founder and former CEO of failed blood testing startup Theranos was found guilty on four out of 11 federal fraud and conspiracy charges.

The verdict comes after a stunning downfall that saw Holmes, once hailed as the next Steve Jobs, go from being a tech industry icon to being a rare Silicon Valley entrepreneur on trial for fraud.

Holmes, inspired by her own fear of needles, started the company at the age of 19, with a mission of creating a cheaper, more efficient alternative to a traditional blood test. Theranos promised patients the ability to test for conditions like cancer and diabetes with just a few drops of blood. It's no surprise that she attracted hundreds of millions of dollars in funding, a board of well-known political figures, and major retail partners.

But what was it like working with this inspirational leader at the start of the journey? We find out from former chief creative officer at Theranos, Patrick O'Neill, who left his job at TBWA/Chiat/Day, the ad agency where he was a creative director, to work alongside CEO Elizabeth Holmes. The following extracts are from an interview given by O'Neill in an interview with Business Insider in June 2023.

I hadn't heard about Theranos before Elizabeth Holmes approached TBWA/Chiat/Day, the ad agency where I was a creative director, in 2012. She really admired Steve Jobs and wanted to model Theranos' branding on the work we'd done with the Apple brand.

We started building the Theranos brand in "stealth mode." It was very secretive.

I'd been working with legacy brands like Visa and the Olympics, and Theranos was the opposite of that — an unknown brand championing a mission to change the healthcare industry.

On top of that, Elizabeth was a female founder, which was incredibly rare for a Silicon Valley startup at that point. She was unlike anyone we'd ever met. Her instincts aligned with what a lot of us believed in — minimalism and clear, purposeful messaging. People now ask me if I found it odd that everything was so secretive, but Theranos was set up very similarly to Apple.

Steve Jobs kept the research and development teams separate. People who worked with Apple weren't allowed to discuss the projects, and the offices had increased security. Sometimes you would see black boxes being carried through the office with the latest version of a new product.

To me, the secrecy was part of working with companies developing groundbreaking technologies. Working closely with Holmes, I felt like she had to bring herself down to earth to communicate with me. I saw her as a brilliant visionary. All her quirks and relentless focus on the mission just confirmed that image to me.

We'd worked with Elizabeth for around a year when the website went live in fall 2013. At the same time, Theranos announced its partnership with Walgreens, which was covered by The Wall Street Journal.

Six months later, Elizabeth asked me to become the chief creative officer at Theranos. I didn't hesitate. Joining a startup was risky, but working for a company that could make the world a better place was too appealing to pass up. It's not every day that your life intersects with someone like Elizabeth or the chance to fulfil a purpose with that intensity.

Elizabeth had very good taste for a client. She was very curious about marketing — she was always asking questions. I appreciated that she wanted to understand it from our perspective. I joined in June 2014.

In the beginning, it was my dream job. Working as the internal creative lead, I had the opportunity to express my creativity across multiple channels. Elizabeth and I met weekly, sometimes more if we were working on an extensive campaign or event.

I helped design the office space, internal communications, the brand, and magazine shoots. For our first advertising campaign, I brought on Errol Morris, a world-famous documentary filmmaker, and Martin Schoeller, the award-winning photographer.

Everything happened under Elizabeth's incredibly close direction. She loved choosing the photographs for campaigns, and we'd spend hours discussing a specific shot. It was enjoyable to work with someone who appreciated the nuances of these things. I went to work believing I was making accessible, affordable healthcare possible. We were consistently reminded of why we were there and what we were working toward.

The company culture discouraged people from discussing what they were working on. Most teams worked in silos, and you weren't allowed in different parts of the building.

Around the time I joined, Elizabeth's infamous Fortune cover came out. The media fell in love with her story.

The first year and a half of working at Theranos was filled with magazine covers, great press, raising money, and getting FDA approval. All these milestones reinforced that this company could change the face of healthcare. In September

2015, Elizabeth was on the cover of Forbes magazine for a profile of her as the youngest self-made female billionaire.

When The Wall Street Journal article came out a month later criticizing the Theranos lab tests, it was unexpected but not surprising. Elizabeth had prepared us to see criticism or naysayers as a natural part of building a cutting-edge business. From late 2015 onward, Elizabeth and I didn't meet as often. When we did, we focused on damage control and protecting the brand's image.

It became normalised that there would be constant accusations. There were town halls where Elizabeth would acknowledge the criticisms coming out in the press, but she was always defiant. These meetings were meant to be bonding experiences, and she would say: "Hey, I know this is hard, but it comes with the territory."

Her narrative was that we were being targeted by the healthcare-industrial complex, or because she was a woman, or the media was tearing Theranos down for sport. I definitely bought into it. In hindsight, the counternarratives seemed defensive. I think there was a little bit inside all of us thinking: "What's going on here?" But we were actively kept from knowing what was really going on.

The labs and wellness centres shut down in Arizona in July 2016. Layoffs happened in October. I was one of the only people left on the creative side. I left at the beginning of 2017... I'd taken a risk, and it hadn't paid off. I had to accept that and move on.

Elizabeth Holmes and the Theranos story are now so well-known that when people ask me what my story is, I have to decide whether I'm going to talk about it. Once I mention it, everyone is pulling up a chair. I don't try to distance myself from Theranos because I was a very public advocate for a long time. Now I just have to take responsibility for my choice and learn from the experience.

I try to focus on the lessons I've learned and to be more sceptical. I've also learned to completely distrust Silicon Valley's "fake it until you make it" mentality. That rhetoric is just a way to condone lying to people.

Everyone was duped, and there were no complicit partners. We were all being blindly led by Elizabeth and her vision of what Theranos could be. For someone who worked at a company where people were doing horrible, illegal things, seeing those people be brought to justice is a comfort.

So, there you have it from Patrick's own account; a company built on the inspiration of one leader who was a genuine radiator. So what actually happened? We followed the timeline from new reports to build up a picture of Elizabeth's downfall.

March 2004: Holmes drops out of Stanford to pursue Theranos

Holmes, a Stanford University sophomore studying chemical engineering, drops out of school to pursue her startup,

Theranos, which she founded in 2003 at age 19. The name is a combination of the words "therapy" and "diagnosis."

September 2009: Ramesh "Sunny" Balwani joins Theranos as Holmes' right-hand man

Balwani joins as chief operating officer and president of the startup. Balwani, nearly 20 years her senior, met Holmes in 2002 on a trip to Beijing through Stanford University. The two are later revealed to be romantically involved.

September 2013: Holmes opens up about Theranos; announces Walgreens partnership

A decade after first starting the company, Holmes takes the lid off Theranos and courts media attention the same month that Theranos and Walgreens announce they've struck up a long-term partnership. The first Theranos Wellness Center location opens in a Walgreens in Palo Alto where consumers can access Theranos' blood test.

The original plan had been to make Theranos' testing available at Walgreens locations nationwide.

September 2014: Holmes named one of the richest women in America by Forbes

Holmes is named to the magazine's American billionaire list with the outlet reporting she owns a 50% stake in the startup, pinning her personal wealth at $4.5 billion.

December 2014: Theranos has raised $400 million

Theranos has raised more than $400 million, according to a profile of the company and Holmes by The New Yorker. It counts Oracle's Larry Ellison among its investors.

July 2015: Theranos gets FDA approval for Herpes test

The FDA clears Theranos to use of its proprietary tiny blood-collection vials to finger stick blood test for herpes simplex 1 virus – its first and only approval for a diagnostic test.

October 2015: Theranos is the subject of a Wall Street Journal investigation; Holmes hits back

The Wall Street Journal reports Theranos is using its proprietary technique on only a small number of the 240 tests it performs, and that the vast majority of its tests are done with traditional vials of blood drawn from the arm, not the "few drops" taken by a finger prick. In response, Theranos defends its testing practices, calling the Journal's reporting "factually and scientifically erroneous."

A day later, Theranos halts the use of its blood-collection vials for all but the herpes test due to pressures from the FDA. (Later that month, the FDA released two heavily redacted reports citing 14 concerns, including calling the company's proprietary vial an "uncleared medical device.")

One week after the Journal report, Holmes is interviewed on-stage at the outlet's conference in Laguna Beach. "We know what we're doing and we're very proud of it," she says.

Amid the criticism, Theranos reportedly shakes up its board of directors, eliminating Henry Kissinger and George Shultz as directors while moving them to a new board of counsellors; the company also forms a separate medical board.

November 2015: Theranos and Safeway partnership falls short

Safeway, which invested $350 million into building out clinics in hundreds of its supermarkets to eventually offer Theranos blood tests, reportedly looks to dissolve its relationship with the company before it ever offered its services.

January 2016: Federal regulators take issue with Theranos' California lab; Walgreens pulls back

Centres for Medicare and Medicaid Services (CMS) sends Theranos a letter saying its California lab has failed to comply with federal standards and that patients are in "immediate jeopardy." It gives the company 10 days to address the issues.

In response, Walgreens says it will not send any lab tests to Theranos' California lab for analysis and suspends Theranos services at its Palo Alto Walgreens location.

March 2016: CMS threatens to ban Holmes, Balwani from lab business

CMS threatens to ban Holmes and Balwani from the laboratory business for two years after the company allegedly failed to fix problems at its California lab. Theranos says that's a "worst case scenario."

May 2016: Balwani steps down; Theranos voids two years of blood tests

Balwani departs. The company also adds three new board members as part of the restructuring: Fabrizio Bonanni, a former executive vice president of biotech firm Amgen, former CDC director William Foege, and former Wells Fargo CEO Richard Kovacevich.

Theranos voids two years of blood test results from its proprietary testing devices, correcting tens of thousands of blood-test reports, the Journal reports.

June 2016: Holmes net worth revised to $0; Theranos loses its largest retail partner

Forbes revises its estimate of Holmes' net worth from $4.5 billion to $0. The magazine also lowers its valuation for the company from $9 billion to $800 million.

Walgreens, once Theranos' largest retail partner, ends its partnership with the company and says it will close all 40 Theranos Wellness Centres.

July 2016: Holmes is banned from running labs for two years

CMS revokes Theranos' license to operate its California lab and bans Holmes from running a blood-testing lab for two years.

August 2016: The company unveils 'miniLab' device

Holmes tries to move past recent setbacks by unveiling a mini testing laboratory, called miniLab, at a conference for the American Association for Clinical Chemistry. In selling the device, versus operating its own clinics, Theranos seeks to effectively side-step CMS sanctions, which don't prohibit research and development.

October 2016: Theranos investor sues the company; Theranos downsizes

Theranos investor Partner Fund Management sues the company for $96.1 million, the amount it sunk into the company in February 2014, plus damages. It accuses the company of securities fraud. Theranos and Partner Fund Management settled in May, 2017, for an undisclosed amount.

The company also lays off 340 employees as it closes clinical labs and wellness centres as it attempts to pivot and focus on the miniLab.

November 2016: Walgreens sues Theranos

Walgreens sues the blood testing startup for breach of contract. Walgreens sought to recover the $140 million it poured into the company. The lawsuit was settled August, 2017.

January 2017: More layoffs, followed by a failed lab inspection

Theranos downsizes its workforce yet again following the increased scrutiny into its operations, laying off approximately 155 employees or about 41% of staffers.

The Wall Street Journal reports that Theranos failed a second regulatory lab inspection in September, and that the company was closing its last blood testing location as a result.

April 2017: Theranos settles with CMS, and Arizona AG

Theranos settles with the CMS, agreeing to pay $30,000 and to not to own or operate any clinical labs for two years.

Theranos also settles with the Arizona Attorney General Mark Brnovich over allegations that its advertisements misrepresented the method, accuracy, and reliability of its blood testing and that the company was out of compliance with federal regulations governing clinical lab testing. Theranos agrees to pay $4.65 million back to its Arizona customers as part of a settlement deal.

March 2018: Holmes charged with massive fraud

The SEC charges Holmes and Balwani with a "massive fraud" involving more than $700 million from investors through an "elaborate, years-long fraud in which they exaggerated or made false statements about the company's technology, business, and financial performance."

The SEC alleges Holmes and Balwani knew that Theranos' proprietary analyzer could perform only 12 of the 200 tests it published on its patient testing menu.

Theranos and Holmes agree to resolve the claims against them, and Holmes gives up control of the company and much of her stake in it. Balwani, however, is fighting the charges, with his attorney saying he "accurately represented Theranos to investors to the best of his ability."

May 2018: "Bad Blood"

Reporter John Carreyrou, who first broke open the story of Theranos for the Wall Street Journal, publishes "Bad Blood," a definitive look at what happened inside the disgraced company. Director Adam McKay (who directed "The Big Short") secures the rights to make the film, starring Jennifer Lawrence as Holmes, by the same name.

June 2018: Holmes and Balwani indicted on criminal fraud charges

Holmes and Balwani are indicted on federal wire fraud charges over allegedly engaging in a multi-million-dollar scheme to defraud investors, as well as a scheme to defraud doctors and patients. Both have pleaded not guilty.

Minutes before the charges were made public, Theranos announced that Holmes has stepped down as CEO. The company's general counsel, David Taylor, takes over as CEO. Holmes remains chair of the company's board.

September 2018: Theranos to dissolve

Taylor emails shareholders that Theranos will dissolve, according to a report from The Wall Street Journal. Taylor said more than 80 potential buyers were not interested in a sale. "We are now out of time," Taylor wrote.

March 2019: Theranos gets the documentary treatment

Alex Gibney, the prolific documentary filmmaker behind "Dirty Money," "Enron: The Smartest Guys in the Room," and "The Armstrong Lie," debuts "The Inventor" on HBO, following the rise and fall of Theranos.

September 2020: Holmes' possible defence strategy comes to light

A new court document reveals Holmes may seek a "mental disease" defense in her criminal fraud trial. Later, in August 2021, unsealed court documents reveal Holmes is likely to claim she was the victim of a decade-long abusive relationship with Balwani. The allegations led to the severing of their trials.

December 2020: Holmes' criminal trial delayed until 2021

Initially set to begin in July 2020, Holmes' criminal trial is further delayed until July 2021 due to the coronavirus pandemic.

March 2021: Holmes' pregnancy further delays trial

News surfaces that Holmes' is expecting her first child, once more further delaying her criminal trial. Holmes' counsel advised the US government that Holmes is due in July 2021, a court document revealed. She gave birth in July.

August 2021: Holmes' criminal trial begins with jury selection

More than 80 potential jurors are brought into a San Jose courtroom for questioning over the course of two days to determine if they are fit to serve as impartial, fair jurors for the criminal trial of Holmes. A jury of seven men and five women is selected, with five alternatives.

December 2021: Jury begins deliberating her fate

After three months of testimony from 32 witnesses, the criminal fraud case of Theranos founder Elizabeth Holmes makes its way to the jury of eight men and four women who will decide her fate. The jury would go on to deliberate for more than 50 hours before returning a verdict.

January 2022: Holmes found guilty on four of 11 federal charges

Holmes is found guilty of one count of conspiracy to defraud investors as well as three wire fraud counts tied to specific investors. She is found not guilty on three additional charges concerning defrauding patients and one charge of conspiracy to defraud patients. The jury returns no verdict on three of the charges concerning defrauding investors. Holmes faces up to 20 years in prison as well as a fine of $250,000 plus restitution for each count.

March 2022: After Hulu miniseries debuts, Balwani's criminal trial kicks off

"The Dropout," a scripted miniseries about Theranos produced by ABC, debuts on Hulu. Amanda Seyfried stars as Holmes and Naveen Andrews plays Balwani. Their romantic and professional relationship features prominently in the show.

Following delays due to Holmes' prolonged trial then a surge of Covid-19, jury selection for Balwani's trial gets underway. On March 22, opening arguments are held and the government's first witness, a former Theranos employee turned whistleblower, is called to the stand.

July 2022: Balwani guilty of federal fraud

After four full days of deliberations, a jury finds Balwani guilty of ten counts of federal wire fraud and two counts of conspiracy to commit wire fraud. Like Holmes, Balwani faces up to 20 years in prison as well as a fine of $250,000 plus restitution for each count of wire fraud and each conspiracy count.

September 2022: Holmes asks for new trial, says a key witness expressed regrets

Holmes asks for a new trial after claiming that a key witness visited her house unannounced and allegedly said he "feels guilty" about his testimony.

In a court filing with the United States District Court for the Northern District of California, Holmes' attorneys said Adam Rosendorff, a former Theranos lab director who was one of the government's main witnesses, arrived at her home on August 8 asking to speak with her. According to the filing, Rosendorff did not interact with Holmes but did speak to her partner Billy Evans, who recounted the exchange in an email to Holmes' lawyers shortly after.

"His shirt was untucked, his hair was messy, his voice slightly trembled," Evans wrote about Rosendorff. According to Evans' email, Rosendorff "said when he was called as a witness he tried to answer the questions honestly but that the prosecutors tried to make everybody look bad."

The former Theranos lab director also "said he felt like he had done something wrong," Evans wrote.

October 2022: Rosendorff takes the stand again

Rosendorff takes the stand again to address concerns from Holmes' defense team and their claims he had shown up at her home after the trial concluded asking to speak with her and expressed regrets about his testimony.

At the hearing, Rosendorff reaffirmed the truthfulness of his testimony at Holmes' trial and said that the government did not influence what he said.

November 2022: Request for new trial is denied

A federal judge denies Elizabeth Holmes' request for a new trial, according to court filings, paving the way for the founder of failed blood testing startup Theranos to be sentenced later in the month.

What can we learn from this epic fall from grace?

The fall from grace of former Theranos CEO Elizabeth Holmes offers several critical lessons both for business and life:

1. **Ethical Integrity:** The case of Elizabeth Holmes underscores the importance of upholding ethical integrity in business practices. Holmes and Theranos faced significant legal and ethical repercussions due to misleading claims and misrepresentation of their technology's capabilities. In life, it pays to be honest and truthful.

2. **Transparency and Accountability:** The downfall of Theranos emphasises the necessity of transparency and accountability in all aspects of business operations, especially in industries where public health and safety are at stake. Open communication and a commitment to accountability are essential for maintaining trust with stakeholders and maintaining the respect of your friends and family.

3. **Due Diligence in Innovation:** Theranos claimed to offer groundbreaking health technology, but the cautionary tale of Elizabeth Holmes highlights the

importance of rigorous, independent validation and due diligence in technological innovation, particularly in regulated industries such as healthcare.

4. **Leadership and Culture:** The leadership and organisational culture at Theranos played a pivotal role in the company's downfall. Learning from this, business leaders must prioritise fostering an environment that encourages transparency, ethical conduct, and a commitment to compliance and integrity

5. **Media and Public Perception:** The media scrutiny and public attention surrounding the Theranos scandal underline the significance of managing public perception and external communication. Companies need to be proactive in addressing any concerns or doubts to protect their reputation and maintain public trust.

These lessons derived from Elizabeth Holmes' and Theranos' downfall serve as cautionary insights for corporate governance, technological innovation, and ethical business conduct in today's challenging business landscape.

VII A STRATEGY FOR BUSINESS RELIANT ON PEOPLE

"You don't build a business – you build people – and then people build the business." Zig Ziglar

The Purpose of a People Strategy

The primary aims of a people strategy are to improve employee performance, motivation, and engagement by fostering a positive work culture. It's about ensuring everyone understands their role, feels appreciated, and possesses the tools necessary for success. By focusing on these goals, you are positioning yourself and your team for sustained business success.

What is The Difference Between People Strategy and Human Resources?

You may be curious about how a people strategy differs from traditional HR practices. While HR typically handles day-to-day administrative duties such as payroll, benefits, and compliance, a people strategy is more strategic and forward-looking. It involves considering the broader perspective—how can we develop our workforce to tackle future challenges? How can we cultivate a culture that appeals to top talent? It is a proactive approach rather than a reactive one.

For instance, let's consider a standard employee lifecycle. This encompasses everything from when your employee first joins your organisation to when they bid farewell.

Why You Need a People Strategy for Your Onboarding Success

When it comes to onboarding, HR typically handles the practical aspects, such as on-the-job training. However, a people strategy can take it a step further by engaging in regular feedback sessions with employees to understand their training experience and make adjustments based on their needs, expectations and input. It makes sense that by making onboarding more collaborative, people feel part of the business rather than a small cog.

Unlock the Power of a People Strategy

A people strategy is crucial because your employees are your most valuable asset. It serves as a roadmap that details how you will attract, nurture, and retain talent, ensuring that your company culture aligns with your business objectives.

According to the Qualtrics Employee Experience Report, only 38% of new employees who had been with their company for six months or less expressed intentions to stay with the company for the next three years, compared to 65% of longer-term employees. This highlights the significance of motivating employees right from the beginning!

Developing and Retaining Top Talent: Building a Future-Proof People Strategy

In the fast-paced and ever-evolving world of business management, nurturing and retaining top talent is a key ingredient for sustained success. By promoting from within and implementing a well-crafted people strategy, organisations can lay the groundwork for employee growth and advancement.

A people strategy that fosters talent involves providing clear and transparent pathways for the professional development of employees. This can encompass personalised development plans, regular check-ins, and opportunities for additional training and mentorship. When employees perceive a tangible career trajectory and avenues for personal growth, their motivation to excel and remain committed to the organisation is significantly amplified.

Prioritising Employee Wellness

Creating a supportive employee experience extends beyond just professional growth. Implementing wellness programs that emphasise the health and well-being of employees can make a profound impact. This can range from offering gym memberships, providing mental health support, to even a simple gesture like fresh fruit in the office or break rooms. The tangible demonstration of care for employee well-being not only fosters loyalty but also builds a positive organisational culture.

In one of my roles at McCann, every Friday afternoon saw the appearance of The Chocolate Trolley; Free Chocolate for everyone in the office! Whilst this served as a fun and motivating treat, it also increased office attendance on a day when most agencies suffered extended lunches or afternoon absence.

It is also worth actively considering employees' personal time and offering flexible working hours that can contribute to a healthier work-life balance, thereby reducing the risk of burnout and enhancing productivity. Simply put, when employees feel valued and supported beyond their professional roles, they are more inclined to contribute their best efforts.

Building A Future-Proof Strategy: Real-Life Inspirations

Drawing insight from real-world examples can provide valuable inspiration for crafting a resilient people strategy.

Successful organisations recognise the importance of internal promotion and fostering strong leadership from within. Establishing clear pathways for career advancement, providing mentorship opportunities, and showcasing instances of successful internal promotions can drive employee motivation and organisational prowess. Adobe's commitment to cultivating a strong learning culture serves as a powerful illustration of this approach. Many initiatives that Adobe implement include:

Leveraging Technology: While the human aspect of a people strategy is crucial, integrating technology for data analysis can augment its effectiveness. By leveraging data to understand employee engagement and sentiments, organisations can tailor their strategies with greater precision and holistic insight.

Fostering a Welcoming and Inclusive Environment: Prioritising diversity, equity, and inclusion (DEI) initiatives is pivotal for fostering an inclusive workplace. Using data-driven methods like anonymous surveys and feedback sessions can more accurately gauge the needs of specific teams and drive meaningful change.

Supporting Remote and Hybrid Work: The rise of remote and hybrid work arrangements necessitates a concerted effort to ensure that all employees feel equally connected and supported. Learning from trailblazers like Automattic, an American global distributed company founded in 2005 and most notable for open source blogging software WordPress, which emphasises social communication and community-building initiatives for remote workers, can provide invaluable insights.

The Five Steps to Crafting a People Strategy

Creating a people strategy is fundamentally about recognising your employees as unique individuals. To assist you in this vital task, we've compiled a straightforward guide to navigate the process effectively.

Step One: Define Your Objectives

To begin, clarify what you hope to achieve with your people strategy. Are you aiming to enhance employee engagement, reduce staff turnover, or foster a more inclusive workplace culture? Whatever your ambitions, it's crucial to articulate your goals with precision.

Next, gather relevant data. Examine turnover rates, engagement scores, and performance metrics. This will provide a clearer picture of your current situation and highlight areas in need of improvement.

Seek out trends and patterns within the data. Are certain departments experiencing higher turnover? Is employee engagement dipping during specific times of the year?

Step Two: Establish Clear Objectives

Identify the key issues that require attention. If you observe a significant number of employees departing within their first year, that signals a potential problem. Based on these insights, formulate specific, measurable objectives. For instance, you might aim to reduce turnover by 10% over the coming year or increase engagement scores by 15%.

Step Three: Solicit Employee Feedback

Engage your employees in the process. Utilise surveys, focus groups, and one-on-one discussions to gather their insights on experiences, challenges, and suggestions for improvement. Compile the feedback to identify common themes and critical areas for enhancement. It's essential to demonstrate that their contributions matter. When employees see their input shaping the new strategy, they are likely to feel more invested and motivated to embrace the changes.

Step Four: Communicate the Strategy

Organise a launch meeting to unveil the new strategy. Clearly outline the goals, the steps needed to achieve them, and how each individual's role contributes to the overall vision. Consider using charts, graphs, and infographics to make the strategy easily digestible at a glance. Be candid about the challenges you face and how the strategy intends to address them. Transparency fosters trust and encourages buy-in from the entire team.

Step Five: Embrace Continuous Adaptation

Consistently seek feedback to assess what's working and what isn't. If something proves ineffective, don't hesitate to make adjustments—it's vital to remain flexible and regularly review the entire strategy. Celebrate your successes, learn from setbacks, and continually refine your approach to ensure it remains effective and relevant.

By taking these steps, you can build a people strategy that not only meets the needs of your organisation but also nurtures and values each employee as an integral part of your team.

Profiling Team Members for the Best Possible Mix

As your business expands, you'll inevitably find yourself needing more people, which brings into play both 'Drains' and 'Radiators'. To maximise the potential of your teams, adopting Profiling Platforms can be a game-changer. These tools help identify overriding strengths and weaknesses, guiding you on who might work best with whom.

There's a range of popular people profiling tools that businesses are using today to pinpoint team strengths and weaknesses. While you should explore which options best suit your needs, here's a selection of the most notable:

DISC: This personal assessment tool is employed by over a million people each year to enhance teamwork, communication, and productivity in the workplace.

Organisations and facilitators use these profiles to spark cultural change, inspiring lasting behavioural shifts that positively impact their workforce.

Myers-Briggs: This renowned system comprises four pairs of preferences, reflecting various personality facets—how we direct and receive energy through Extraversion (E) or Introversion (I), process information via Sensing (S) or Intuition (N), make decisions with Thinking (T) or Feeling (F), and engage with the world through Judging (J) or Perceiving (P). Most individuals resonate with one preference in each pair, revealing their natural tendencies and comfort zones outside of their roles. By combining these letters, we uncover 16 distinct personality types, each with unique characteristics.

StrengthsFinder (CliftonStrengths): This tool identifies an individual's top strengths from 34 themes, empowering teams to appreciate each member's unique contributions.

Big Five Personality Traits (OCEAN): This model evaluates individuals across five dimensions: Openness, Conscientiousness, Extraversion, Agreeableness, and Neuroticism, offering a comprehensive perspective on personality.

16 Personality Factor Questionnaire (16PF): Created by Raymond Cattell, this tool assesses 16 different personality traits and is frequently utilised in professional environments for recruitment and development.

Thomas-Kilmann Conflict Mode Instrument (TKI): This tool evaluates how individuals handle conflict, helping teams navigate disagreements more effectively.

Cultural Values Assessment (CVA): This tool assists organisations in understanding the values that underpin their culture, which can significantly influence team dynamics and performance.

Utilising these tools can foster improved communication, collaboration, and productivity within teams, even amidst a blend of drains and radiators. By leveraging individual strengths and addressing weaknesses, the dynamics of a team can be significantly enhanced through a deeper understanding of individual profiles.

Building a Dream Team to Elevate Your Business

You may be exceptional at your craft, but in the long run, that talent alone won't suffice if you can't build a fantastic team around you.

Your startup could be just what your community needs, yet if your team members struggle to collaborate, it's destined to falter. Even if you're thrilled to be promoted to team leader, without cultivating trust among your colleagues, achieving your team goals will remain elusive.

The old adage, "Teamwork makes the dream work," rings ever true. A harmonious group can create something remarkable from the ground up. Together, you can leverage each other's strengths to accomplish feats that would be impossible alone. Bringing people together might seem straightforward, but crafting a truly successful team requires skill. If you're keen to learn how to build a team, recognise that every great collaboration begins with a talented, motivated leader.

Such a leader knows how to channel each team member's abilities, enabling you all to reach for your most ambitious goals. If you aspire to be an effective leader and discover how to assemble a dream team, you're in the right place. It's undoubtedly a journey, but we're here to guide you through nine actionable strategies for team building.

The Importance of Teamwork

Teamwork is the oft-overlooked catalyst that propels every successful business forward. Without a well-coordinated team, a company may never realise its full potential.

Every individual on your team has the capacity to contribute their unique skills and talents, but it's teamwork that truly unlocks that potential. Research backs this up. A recent study found that 50% of organisations surveyed attributed their ability to meet operational goals to effective employee teamwork. This highlights a critical reality: the other 50% were still grappling with their objectives, underscoring the significance of a cohesive team.

Simply grouping your employees won't yield results if the team lacks clear goals. They need defined objectives and specific individual responsibilities to thrive. When your team is aligned, it can lead to extraordinary outcomes for your business. In fact, employees who frequently collaborate are often more engaged, more successful in reaching their goals, and experience less fatigue.

Teamwork also has the remarkable ability to enhance your employees' well-being, fostering a sense of connection among them. When your team is happy and productive, your business is bound to flourish.

Collaboration encourages employees to think about the bigger picture they wish to achieve. With a common goal in sight, they're more likely to work together rather than against one another. Teamwork can also dissolve barriers between departments and smaller teams. By understanding one another better, everyone within the company can perform their roles more effectively.

Finally, teamwork is essential because it creates valuable learning opportunities. Junior employees can gain insights from collaborating with their more experienced counterparts, while senior team members can refine their leadership skills and learn how to cultivate an effective team. Ultimately, this fosters career growth for everyone involved, which is a brilliant way to enhance employee retention.

Six Characteristics of a Successful Team

Exceptional teams share a few key traits. If you're keen to learn how to construct a high-performing team, understanding these characteristics is a fantastic starting point.

Here are six hallmarks of a successful team:

1. Effective communication among all team members
2. Diverse individuals who offer various perspectives and skills
3. A willingness to learn and adapt to change
4. A clear understanding of the company culture
5. A leadership style that promotes accountability and support
6. A goal-oriented mindset

How to Build a Really Strong Team

Creating a great team requires dedication and effort. Remember to be patient and consistent—over time, you'll discover how to assemble your dream team. Keep your focus on one overarching objective: uniting an incredible group of people towards a common goal.

Ready to embark on this journey? Here are nine ways to cultivate that really strong team you need for success:

Establish Company Culture

Your new team needs clarity about expectations, so it's essential to define the company culture you wish to uphold from the outset. This will guide your team in their behaviour and approach to work.

Don't forget your role as a leader—facilitating these values will help ensure everyone stays aligned.

Define Roles and Responsibilities

For your team to function effectively, each member must understand their individual responsibilities. While teamwork is collaborative, independent work is also crucial for seamless operations.

Avoid confusion about roles; ensure your team knows what they are meant to accomplish. It's equally important that they know whom to approach for resolving conflicts or queries about their tasks.

Ensure Everyone Feels Respected

At every level, team members should feel valued as both employees and individuals. They are not just cogs in a machine; their personal lives, feelings, and unique qualities contribute to who they are.

Show respect by acknowledging the whole person. This recognition boosts confidence and well-being, which can enhance productivity—beneficial for the business.

Stay Organised, don't get side-tracked

Effective leaders are organised. They prioritise team management and regularly check in on progress.

From the moment you start building your team, implement organisational processes and project management systems. This will help prevent overwhelm and drive your team's success.

Encourage Your Team Members

A motivating work environment fosters success. Maintain a positive atmosphere to inspire growth among your team.

When mistakes occur, approach them constructively rather than with punishment. Help your team identify learning opportunities from these experiences—this demonstrates your commitment to their personal development.

Communicate Openly

Effective communication keeps teams connected and aligned. In contrast, a silent team risks disintegration. If a problem arises, address it with your team and invite their thoughts.

Found a solution? Share it. Have important updates to convey? Communicate clearly and allow time for questions. The more dialogue there is, the more collaborative and comfortable your team will become.

Be Open to Feedback (*any* feedback)

We can't improve without reflecting on our mistakes. Even in the absence of issues, constructive criticism and thorough feedback promote growth.

Plus, it can prevent future problems. When receiving feedback, remember to listen actively.

When both leaders and team members embrace feedback, they become better equipped to tackle challenges. This is one of the best ways to learn how to build an effective team for the long haul.

Celebrate Achievements

Teamwork deserves recognition. Keep an eye out for excellent performances and don't hesitate to commend them. Some goals may be hard for individuals to reach but can be easily achieved as a team.

Acknowledging your team's hard work cultivates an environment that encourages risk-taking and ambition. Even if they stumble, they'll know they have a supportive team behind them.

Value Diversity

Collaborating with individuals from different backgrounds and experiences enriches your business.

Rather than diminishing what makes your employees unique, celebrate it. This fosters an environment where team members feel safe to be their authentic selves.

Your next step

Knowing how to build a team doesn't happen overnight. Even a group of the most talented people won't immediately know how to work well with each other. It takes time and patience to excel at teamwork.

Along the way, you might have team members who are more difficult to work with. We've already shared our insights into turning Drains into Radiators so don't give up — it is possible to learn how to build a cohesive team. Keep working towards your goal of creating a team that's confident, effective, and can face any challenge that comes their way.

Ultimately, don't forget to do your part and give yourself compassion as you become the best leader you can be.

VIII

A PLAN FOR LIFE WITH LESS STRESS

"Remember that stress doesn't come from what's going on in your life. It comes from your thoughts about what's going on in your life." – Andrew Bernstein

Ditching The Stress For A Life Less Ordinary

I n 2007, a British family took the plunge and left the rat race behind to embrace a life on a desert island—one that was truly remote, over 10,000 miles away. The von Engelbrechten family, comprising Boris and Karyn and their three sons, Jack, Luca, and Felix, traded their familiar comforts for the tiny, idyllic island of Fofoa in Tonga, seeking a simpler, less stressful existence.

You might say every child dreams of endless summers on the beach, and this adventurous couple turned that dream into reality. Imagine moving to an island that takes three days to reach! While they openly acknowledge the challenges of island life, they've made Fofoa their home, a small paradise where they can breathe easy.

Karyn, originally from North Wraxall in Wiltshire, grew weary of spending endless hours commuting on the M4 from her quaint village near Bath to London for her role as an IT manager. Craving a change, she set off on a journey that would transform her life.

It was during her travels that she met Boris, a German hotel manager. Together, they settled on the tiny island, which is just 1km in size. "I had reached a point where most of my life was spent on the M4. I thought, there has to be more than this," Karyn shared on Channel 4's Escape to the Wild.

The couple, who had previously lived in New Zealand, chose Tonga for its tranquillity and have found adventure ever since. Upon arrival, they collaborated with local craftsmen to construct a stunning beachside home using materials sourced from the island, including coral slabs from the shore. Their two-bedroom sanctuary, built for around £70,000, also serves as a guesthouse, complete with a living and dining area. The rainwater that falls on the island is cleverly piped in for drinking, and they proudly claim to be '60 per cent' self-sufficient, growing their own fruits and vegetables.

Every three weeks, a three-hour boat trip brings canned food from a larger island—an essential lifeline in their remote lifestyle. "I wanted my kids to be free and connected to nature," Karyn explains. Growing up in such a breathtaking corner of the world has its perks, but it's not without its challenges, including the occasional hurricane and earthquake.

"We experienced a tsunami about four years ago," Karyn recalls. "I was making breakfast for the boys when I noticed the water wasn't flowing as it usually does—it was moving like a river. We had the highest and lowest tides within just ten minutes. It was a valuable lesson for the boys: if you see that, don't look at it, just get up to the house!"

Living on an island is both thrilling and laid-back, as Karyn's teenage son points out. "It's exciting and fun, but it's also quite slow," he says. "I crave friends; there's really nobody here. I'm mainly heading to New Zealand for that. The school will be different, but there will be so much more to learn."

Meanwhile, Karyn continues to homeschool their other two sons, ensuring they keep pace with their peers back in England. "I make sure they're at the level they should be in England," she affirms.

In this remarkable journey of leaving behind the chaos for a slice of paradise, the von Engelbrechten family embodies the quest for a life filled with adventure, connection, and simplicity.

What is Stress?

Let's explore what stress truly is. Stress is the body's reaction to physical, emotional, or mental pressures. When you experience stress, your body enters a fight-or-flight state, releasing hormones that boost your energy and sharpen your alertness by increasing your heart rate, blood pressure, and blood sugar levels.

In short bursts, stress can actually be beneficial. It can help you dodge an unforeseen obstacle or power through tasks to meet a crucial deadline.

While it's perfectly normal to feel stressed from time to time, living with chronic stress can take a toll on both your mental and physical well-being. If you often find yourself feeling anxious, unsettled, worried, or struggling to sleep, these overwhelming feelings can make life challenging.

There are common traits that distinguish those who are constantly stressed from those who seem more laid-back about everything. Take a moment to reflect on whether you see these characteristics in yourself or your colleagues:

Stressed People	Relaxed People
Feeling nervous or anxious	Feeling calm and collected
Getting angry or frustrated	Being patient and tolerant
Getting upset or crying easily	Being able to regulate emotions
Constantly worrying about something	Not sweating the small stuff
Frequently feeling overwhelmed	Generally feeling confident
Often feeling unable to cope	Having faith in your ability to cope
Feeling like you're losing control	Feeling like you have everything under control

What's the Secret to a Less Stressful Life?

We can't all up sticks and move to a deserted island and so, what mindset should we embrace to reduce the stress in our lives? To uncover this, we need to examine the potential sources of stress. The following list represents the most common causes of daily stress:

Daily Pressures: The demands of family, the challenges of parenting, the rigours of work or study, the frustration of traffic on your commute, and the myriad of everyday responsibilities can all weigh heavily on us.

Life Events: Major transitions like divorce, a significant breakup, the loss of a loved one, serious illness, or job loss can create immense strain.

Traumatic Experiences: Natural disasters, accidents, and other traumatic events that threaten your safety or well-being can leave lasting impacts.

Financial Concerns: Worries about debt, loss of income, economic hardship, or limited access to opportunities can add considerable stress.

Discrimination: Facing bias based on gender, sexual orientation, appearance, race, ethnicity, nationality, language, or immigration status can create ongoing tension.

Social and Environmental Issues: Worries about social injustice, pollution, climate change, and other pressing concerns can also contribute to our stress levels.

When we are under significant stress, the reactions can manifest themselves in many different ways. As a stressed-out person, you may experience various symptoms, including:

Fatigue
Lack of energy
Forgetfulness
Difficulty concentrating
Headaches

Digestive issues
Aches and pains
Frequent illnesses
Stiffness in the neck or jaw
Unplanned weight changes
Sleep disturbances
Increased reliance on substances like alcohol or drugs for relaxation

Over time, chronic stress can keep your hormonal and neurological systems in overdrive, even when you're not in immediate danger. This can lead to or worsen a range of health conditions, such as:

High blood pressure
Heart disease
Diabetes
Obesity
Depression
Anxiety
Skin issues, like acne and eczema
Menstrual problems
Post-traumatic stress disorder

Moreover, a 2017 study revealed that chronic stress can lead to the atrophy of the brain, diminishing its size and impairing memory and cognitive function. It's clear that stress can severely impact your quality of life—and for some, may even shorten it.

It's no wonder we all have an innate desire to reduce stress, and the advantages of doing so are plentiful:

Feeling less tense and anxious

Enjoying a better mood

Experiencing improved sleep

Gaining more control over your weight

Strengthening relationships with family, friends, and colleagues

Cultivating a sense of calm, confidence, and competence

Regaining control over your life

Feeling happier and more fulfilled

By recognising the sources of stress and actively working towards a more relaxed mindset, you can unlock a brighter, more satisfying future.

9 Ways to Reduce Stress

Dr Allison Gaffey, a clinical psychologist at Yale Medicine's Department of Internal Medicine, specialises in addressing the impacts of stress. She claims that there are effective strategies that help you lower your stress levels that lead to a better quality of life.

Identify Your Stressors: Understanding the factors, situations, and people that negatively affect you is essential for transforming those dynamics and better managing your stress. Consider keeping a journal to record your stress triggers and your reactions.

Enhance Your Time Management Skills: Improving your ability to manage time can help you handle your responsibilities more effectively. Try planning ahead, prioritising tasks based on importance, allocating time realistically, eliminating distractions, and resisting the urge to procrastinate.

Get Active: Choose activities you enjoy and aim for between 150 and 300 minutes of exercise each week. Regular physical activity not only reduces stress but also enhances your capacity to cope with stressful situations. Plus, it boosts your mood and fosters better overall health.

Connect with Loved Ones: Spend quality time with family and friends and share your concerns with them. Social connections can alleviate stress, enhance your sense of belonging, improve both mental and physical health, and elevate your overall well-being.

Practice Relaxation Techniques: Engaging in relaxation exercises, such as meditation, can help calm your racing thoughts and bring you into the present moment.

Limit Technology Use: While staying informed is important, constant exposure to negative news on social media or television can be distressing. Consider restricting your television viewing to just 10 minutes a day and checking social media accounts infrequently.

Maintain a Healthy Routine: Focus on eating a balanced diet and getting ample sleep. A consistent routine can mitigate stress, while erratic schedules, lack of sleep, and poor nutrition can exacerbate it.

Avoid Substances for Relief: Steer clear of alcohol, smoking, vaping, or illegal drugs as a means to cope with stress. Instead, engage in hobbies and activities you love to help you unwind.

Seek Professional Help: If you frequently feel overwhelmed and struggle to cope, consulting a mental health professional can be beneficial. They can assist you in identifying your stress triggers and equip you with valuable coping skills.

By incorporating these strategies into your life, you can create a more peaceful and fulfilling existence.

Healthy Coping Skills for Uncomfortable Emotions

Whether you've been let go by a partner or had a particularly challenging day at work, having effective coping skills can be crucial for navigating tough times. These skills help you endure, diminish, and manage the stresses life throws your way.

Coping skills are essentially the strategies we employ to handle stressful situations. By mastering your stress management, you can improve both your physical and mental well-being, which in turn enhances your ability to perform at your best.

However, not all coping skills are equally beneficial. It can be tempting to resort to quick fixes that offer immediate relief but may lead to larger issues later on. Establishing healthy coping mechanisms is essential for alleviating emotional distress and addressing the stressful situations you encounter. Here are some examples of healthy coping skills:

- Setting and maintaining boundaries
- Practising relaxation techniques such as deep breathing, meditation, and mindfulness
- Engaging in regular physical activity
- Creating to-do lists and setting achievable goals

In this chapter, we'll delve into coping skills that can assist you in managing stress and overcoming challenges. Discover how various strategies, including problem-focused and emotion-focused skills, can be most effective.

Problem-Based vs. Emotion-Based Coping

There are five primary types of coping skills: problem-focused coping, emotion-focused coping, religious coping, meaning-making, and social support.

Among these, problem-focused coping and emotion-focused coping are particularly significant. Understanding their differences can help you identify the most suitable strategy for your circumstances.

Problem-focused coping is particularly useful when you need to alter your situation, perhaps by eliminating a source of stress from your life. For instance, if you find yourself in an unhealthy relationship, the most effective way to alleviate your anxiety and sadness might be to end that relationship rather than merely soothing your emotions.

On the other hand, emotion-focused coping is beneficial when you need to manage your feelings, especially when you either prefer not to change your situation or when certain circumstances are beyond your control. For example, if you are mourning the loss of a loved one, it's vital to address your emotions in a healthy manner, as the situation itself cannot be altered.

Finding Your Best Coping Strategy

There isn't always a one-size-fits-all solution for coping. Ultimately, it's up to you to determine which coping skill is most likely to be effective for your circumstances. We've explored a few scenarios where you might find yourself feeling derailed, leading to negative thoughts and stress, despite your best efforts. In these scenarios, we have the opportunity to explore problem or emotion focused responses, both of which can act as a coping strategy. In a perfect world, we would explore both and decide our best approach before negative thoughts turn to stress.

Being dumped by your partner

You thought it was going well, after all it's been several months of fun and adventure, but what you thought was a simple coffee invite turns out to you being dumped. To make it worse, you're in a public space and you now feel like screaming, crying, throwing your coffee cup across the room or all three.

Problem-focused coping: Rather than begging for another chance, sympathise with their situation, after all it can't be easy for them to end a relationship this way. Ask them for their real reasons for the decision, not the kind excuse but the real reason. It's your chance to be calm and reasonable, if they are too upset to dig deep, ask them to think about it and send you a message by text or email, explaining that you value self-improvement and you owe it to your next partner.

This problem-focused response may enable you to identify some correctable issues that reverse their decision especially after you played the 'next partner' card. Even if it doesn't, you might learn some valuable insight about your own shortcomings.

Emotion-focused coping: To avoid your emotions spilling over, you make your excuses and leave ordering your favourite 'to-go' treat. As soon as you are home, you deflect the negativity by making a list of things you didn't like about your partner, after all, no one's perfect. This serves as a quick fix rationale to coping with the situation.

Reading Your Performance Review

You open your email, and to your astonishment, your annual performance review reveals that you're underperforming in several areas. This news leaves you feeling anxious and frustrated—after all, you thought you were doing well. Ouch!

Problem-focused coping: Rather than dwelling on the negativity, you decide to speak with your manager about ways to enhance your performance. Together, you create a clear plan for improvement, and as a result, you gradually regain your confidence in your ability to succeed.

Emotion-focused coping: During your lunch break, you dive into a captivating book to escape the nagging worry of potential dismissal. After work, a trip to the gym and tidying your living space help lift your spirits, providing you with the clarity needed to face the situation.

Getting a Teenager to Clean aka achieving the near-impossible

You've repeatedly reminded your teenager to tidy their bedroom, but a week has gone by, and clothes and rubbish are piling up. Before you leave for work, you firmly insist they must clean their room after school "or else." Yet, when you return home, you find them glued to their video games amidst the chaos.

Problem-focused coping: You sit down with your teenager and explain that they will be grounded until their room is clean. You confiscate their electronics and impose restrictions. In the meantime, you shut the door to their room to spare yourself from the sight of the mess.

Emotion-focused coping: To calm your nerves, you run a hot bath, knowing that a soak will help you unwind. This moment of relaxation prevents you from overreacting or raising your voice in frustration.

Giving a Presentation

You've received an invitation to present in front of a large audience. Flattered by the opportunity, you eagerly accept, but as the event approaches, your anxiety skyrockets— public speaking is not your strong suit.

Problem-focused coping: You choose to hire a public speaking coach who can help you craft a compelling speech and deliver it with confidence. You practice in front of friends and family, ensuring you feel well-prepared for the big day.

Emotion-focused coping: You reassure yourself that you can handle this challenge. Whenever panic arises, you engage in relaxation exercises, reminding yourself that even if you feel nervous, the audience is unlikely to notice.

Problem-focused coping skills aim to change the situation, while emotion-focused skills focus on altering how you feel. Knowing which approach is right for a specific scenario can significantly enhance your ability to manage stress.

Healthy Emotion-Focused Coping Skills

Whether you're feeling lonely, anxious, sad, or angry, emotion-focused coping skills can help you navigate your feelings in a constructive manner. Healthy coping strategies may soothe you, provide a temporary distraction, or help you tolerate your distress.

Sometimes, facing your emotions head-on is beneficial. For instance, allowing yourself to feel sad after the loss of a loved one can be a way to honour that loss.

While it's important to use coping skills to alleviate some of your distress, these strategies shouldn't revolve around constantly distracting you from reality.

At other times, coping skills can help shift your mood. If you've had a tough day at work, playing with your children or watching a funny film might lift your spirits. Alternatively, if you're feeling angry about something someone said, a healthy coping strategy could give you the space to calm down before you say something you might regret.

Tips for Business and Life:

Life can throw us curveballs, but how we respond can make all the difference. Here are some engaging ways to cope with emotions and pave the path to a more relaxed, fulfilling life:

1. Pamper Yourself: Treat your senses! Indulge in a fragrant lotion, immerse yourself in nature, enjoy a soothing bath, sip on a warm cup of tea, or give yourself a little makeover—whether it's a fresh coat

of nail polish, a stylish hairdo, or a rejuvenating face mask.

2. Dive into a Hobby: Rediscover joy by immersing yourself in activities you love. Whether it's colouring, sketching, or jamming out to your favourite tunes, let your creativity flow and watch your stress melt away.

3. Get Moving: Physical activity is a fantastic stressbuster! Stretch out with some yoga, take a leisurely stroll, hit the trails for a hike, or join a recreational sport. Your body and mind will thank you!

4. Get Things Done: Channel your energy into productive tasks. Tackle that messy closet, whip up a delicious meal, tend to your garden, or lose yourself in a captivating book. Focusing on a task can be incredibly grounding.

5. Practice Mindfulness: Shift your perspective by acknowledging what you're grateful for. Meditate, envision your "happy place," or browse through photos that remind you of joyful moments and cherished connections.

6. Relax and Unwind: Find comfort in playful moments with a pet, practice deep breathing, or squeeze a stress ball to release tension. Explore relaxation apps, enjoy calming scents through aromatherapy, or try progressive muscle relaxation. Journaling can also be a powerful tool for processing your thoughts.

7. Explore Coping Strategies: Consider both problem-focused and emotion-focused approaches to navigate

life's challenges. Weigh your options and decide which method suits your situation best or combine both for a more comprehensive solution.

By incorporating these strategies into your routine, you can cultivate a life filled with positivity and resilience!

IX FAMOUS RADIATORS WE CAN LEARN FROM

"Leaders become great, not because of their power, but because of their ability to empower others" John Maxwell

Leaders Who Changed the World for the Better

L ike empires, companies can rise and fall with the times, but some endure through the ages, and the secret to their longevity lies in exceptional leadership. Great leaders possess the remarkable ability to inspire their teams, help others see and believe in a shared vision, and drive innovation within their organisations. A strong leader at the helm is something every investor, consumer, and employee longs for.

What Is an Industry Leader?

An industry leader is a respected professional with extensive expertise in a particular field. These individuals are innovative, driven, strategic, and adept at adapting to evolving trends. When new technologies emerge or consumer demands shift, they know how to respond effectively and provide valuable solutions.

On an organisational level, business leaders understand how to meet both company and consumer needs. They conduct thorough research on their audience and competitors, delivering strategic solutions that address market and organisational demands.

To achieve this, industry leaders must have a deep understanding of their workforce, insights into competitors' operations, and the ability to offer meaningful solutions that enhance products and services. Their ultimate aim is to transform their companies for the better.

Industry leaders carve out pathways to success with fresh ideas and distinctive approaches. While they can wear many hats, they often take on roles such as CEO, entrepreneur, or company founder.

What Are the Qualities of a Business Leader?

Here are some of the key qualities that define successful industry leaders:

Informed and Innovative: Industry leaders stay ahead of the curve. They continually research trends, analyse the latest advancements in their field, and dedicate time to developing solutions that benefit their organisations.

Goal-Oriented: Professional leaders across all sectors have a clear understanding of their company's objectives, both short and long-term. They possess a detailed vision of what it takes to achieve these goals, laying the groundwork for sustained success.

Exceptional Communication Skills: Industry leaders know how to communicate effectively with board members, employees, and stakeholders to address opportunities and challenges. They prioritise clear communication over vague or abrupt exchanges, articulating their goals and solutions with precision. They also engage in active listening, valuing feedback from others.

Risk-Takers: Every industry requires leaders who are willing to embrace the unknown and take calculated risks. These leaders understand that achieving success often involves striving for both easily attainable goals and longer-term aspirations.

These courageous individuals are unafraid to express their ideas and put them into action, even when faced with the possibility of failure. It is these qualities that distinguish extraordinary business leaders from the rest.

We've selected our favourite five examples of leaders who we can learn from and inspire us to have more control of our business and life. So here they are in no particular order:

Reshma Saujani, founder of Girls Who Code

In 2012, Reshma Saujani launched Girls Who Code in response to the alarming gender gap in entry-level tech roles. Back in 1995, women made up 37% of computer scientists, but 26 years later, that figure has plummeted to a mere 24%.

Recognising that many girls drop out of computer science during their teenage years, Girls Who Code runs various programmes aimed at students aged 13 to 17. The Clubs Programme offers a fun and welcoming environment for students in Years 3 to 12 to explore coding, while the Summer Immersion Programme provides a two-week virtual camp for those in Years 10 to 12. For university students, the College Loops networks help Girls Who Code alumni thrive and connect with fellow women in tech.

Since its inception, Girls Who Code has impacted the lives of 500 million individuals through its programmes, online resources, campaigns, books, and advocacy efforts. In 2019, the organisation was recognised as the Most Innovative Non-Profit by Fast Company.

Who Is Reshma Saujani?

Saujani's impressive educational background includes degrees from the University of Illinois, Harvard's Kennedy School of Government, and Yale Law School. She began her career as a lawyer and activist before making history in 2010 as the first Indian American woman to run for U.S. Congress. During her campaign, visits to local schools revealed a stark gender gap in computing classes, inspiring her to establish Girls Who Code.

Saujani is also an accomplished author, with works such as Women Who Don't Wait in Line, Brave, Not Perfect, and the New York Times bestseller Girls Who Code: Learn to Code and Change the World. Her TED Talk, Teach Girls Bravery, Not Perfection, has garnered millions of views, and she hosts the award-winning podcast Brave, Not Perfect, which empowers women to lead their most courageous and fulfilling lives.

Four Lessons from Saujani's Career for Aspiring Leaders

1. Set Meaningful, Attainable Targets:

To drive real change, organisations need to establish realistic objectives. Leaders often express concern about issues like climate change and diversity, but their words ring hollow if they lack accountability. Girls Who Code, for instance, aims to close the gender gap in new entry-level tech roles by 2030.

Recently, Saujani introduced the Marshall Plan for Moms, designed to address the adverse effects of COVID-19 on women in the workplace. This initiative, proposed to President Biden, advocates for monthly payments of £2,400 for mothers in need, alongside paid family leave, pay equity, affordable childcare, and training programmes. With two years until the midterm elections, Saujani is determined to see this proposal passed.

2. Commit to Diversity, Equity, and Inclusion:

Girls Who Code prides itself on valuing diversity, equity, and inclusion as fundamental to its mission. The organisation recognises that intersectionality can hinder girls from marginalised backgrounds from thriving in tech careers. Notably, nearly half of the girls served by Girls Who Code come from historically underrepresented groups, including low-income families and Black or Latina communities.

3. Pass the Baton:

In February 2021, Saujani announced her decision to step down as CEO of Girls Who Code, with Dr. Tarika Barrett succeeding her in April 2021. Barrett, the former COO, previously worked with New York City's Department of Education, where she helped establish the city's first school dedicated to software engineering.

For many leaders, relinquishing control of a passion project can be daunting. However, fostering innovation and meaningful change often requires recognising the right moment to invite new voices and perspectives. As Saujani stated in an exclusive interview with Forbes, "I believe that leaders cannot stay in organisations forever, and you can't remain innovative with the same person at the helm indefinitely."

4. Never Give Up:

The journey towards equality and justice is often fraught with setbacks. When challenges arise, it's essential for leaders to double down on their efforts. Post-COVID, UNICEF estimates that 20 million secondary school-aged girls could drop out of education. A survey of Girls Who Code alumni revealed that 30% had lost jobs or internships due to the pandemic. Rather than being discouraged, Saujani responded by hosting a virtual hiring summit that attracted 800 women and girls.

How to Lead Like Reshma Saujani

If you're struggling to attract, retain, or empower marginalised women in your organisation, consider these questions:

What meaningful actions am I taking to address inequalities in the workplace? What are my long-term objectives?

Am I educating myself about the impact of discrimination on marginalised employees? How can I amplify their voices?

Can I recognise when it's time to pass the mic?

Am I too quick to abandon my mission when faced with obstacles, or am I committed to my goals?

Am I too quick to abandon my mission when faced with obstacles and pushback, or am I committed to my goals?

Jørgen Vig Knudstorp, Lego Group Chairman

LEGO, founded in 1930 by Danish carpenter Ole Kirk Kristiansen, has blossomed into one of the most beloved toy brands around the globe. The name LEGO is derived from the Danish phrase "leg godt," meaning "play well," perfectly encapsulating the brand's mission to inspire creativity through play.

In 1947, LEGO began producing plastic toys alongside its traditional wooden offerings, and by 1949, the iconic interlocking bricks—originally termed "Automatic Binding Bricks"—were introduced. By 1951, plastic toys accounted for half of LEGO's production. Despite scepticism from industry experts who doubted plastic could ever rival wood, these innovative building blocks became an extraordinary success.

In 1954, Ole's son, Godtfred, stepped into the role of junior managing director. During a dialogue with an international buyer, he envisioned a comprehensive toy system that would enhance play opportunities through greater interchangeability. However, the existing locking mechanism fell short of this vision. In 1958, LEGO patented a new system with the introduction of ABS (acrylonitrile butadiene styrene) polymer. The Duplo series, featuring larger bricks for younger children, launched in 1969, and the iconic LEGO Minifigures made their debut in 1978.

When Jørgen Vig Knudstorp joined the LEGO Group in 2004, the company was grappling with significant challenges. Discover how Knudstorp transformed LEGO into a thriving enterprise.

Who is Jørgen Vig Knudstorp?

Born in 1968 in Fredericia, Denmark, Jørgen Vig Knudstorp pursued his undergraduate degree at Aarhus University. His early career involved research at the university, alongside a master's degree and PhD in economics. He worked as a business consultant from 1998 to 2000 while continuing his academic pursuits. Before joining LEGO in 2001,

Knudstorp was a consultant at McKinsey & Co. By 2004, he became CEO, despite being an outsider in a family-owned business.

At that time, LEGO was losing a staggering £1 million a day, accumulating debt, and overextending into unprofitable areas like branded children's clothing. Knudstorp implemented innovative strategies that revitalised the company, turning losses into profits—multiplying by five.

After successfully rebuilding the brand, Knudstorp stepped down as CEO in 2016, taking on the role of chairman of the LEGO Group, and he was nominated to the Starbucks board of directors in 2017.

Four Key Lessons on Implementing Change from Jørgen Vig Knudstorp:

1. Earn Trust to Lead Effectively

In an interview with Harvard Business Review, Knudstorp shared how he faced the challenge of gaining his employees' trust upon joining LEGO. He emphasised a management style that prioritised open communication and fiscal responsibility. "In Danish, we have a saying that translates as 'managing at eye level,'" he explained, highlighting the importance of engaging with everyone from factory workers to marketers. This approach fostered trust and respect, facilitating the necessary improvements and maintaining morale during tough times.

2. Focus on Core Values

Knudstorp prioritised narrowing LEGO's focus by asking a fundamental question: why does LEGO exist? The team concluded that the goal was to offer core products that help children develop systematic, creative problem-solving skills. They resolved not to chase size but to strive for excellence, shifting from rigid top-down management to a more flexible structure that empowered individual managers.

3. Engage Customers to Build Loyalty

While aligning LEGO's internal team was crucial, Knudstorp recognised the importance of customer engagement. In an interview with Boston Consulting Group, he noted that loyalty had been taken for granted. To better understand customer sentiment, he implemented a Net Promoter score to measure satisfaction and began consulting with adult LEGO fans. This led to collaboration with over 100,000 volunteer product designers, allowing customers to play a more active role in product development.

4. View Your Business as an Ecosystem

Knudstorp advocated for allowing LEGO's various affiliates and partners to operate independently rather than enforcing a one-size-fits-all approach. He believed this autonomy would foster "natural synergies," akin to a healthy ecosystem where diverse entities thrive together.

Leading Like Jørgen Vig Knudstorp

Knudstorp's leadership revitalised a cherished brand. Whether you're steering a large corporation or a small local enterprise, his methods offer valuable insights. Keep these four principles in mind to guide your journey through change, make informed decisions, and set your organisation up for enduring success:

Listen to and learn from your employees. Without their trust and input, you won't be able to lead effectively. Real leadership stems from a well-managed, closely aligned team. Talk to your staff about what they think needs improving, what's working, and how they see the company evolving.

When business isn't going as well as you'd hoped, it's easy to get bogged down in the details. Start big, zeroing in on the ultimate goal or the main problem you're trying to solve, then work your way down. This will help to keep things manageable and focused.

Employee alignment is important, but customer involvement is just as crucial. Today's consumers have more options and information at their disposal than ever before, so it's important to understand their needs, wants, and concerns. Track successes, gather data, and put the customer front and center.

Many businesses have several moving parts, or affiliated offshoots, events, and partnerships. Cohesion is good, but being overly controlling of independent entities can backfire, creating a culture of fear and quashing creativity.

Think more holistically and remember that what works in one corporate office may not translate to another location.

Elon Musk, Tesla CEO and SpaceX Founder

Whether you admire him or critique him, Elon Musk is undeniably a remarkable achiever with valuable lessons for us all. Achieving significant results in both life and business often requires a willingness to embrace risk, a principle that Musk embodies perfectly. As the driving force behind innovations spanning web software, the automotive sector, and even space exploration, his illustrious—and frequently controversial—career is a testament to the power of risk-taking.

While not every gamble pays off, Musk's mindset and approach to risk offer invaluable insights for business leaders everywhere.

Who Is Elon Musk?

Widely recognised as the founder of Tesla, Elon Musk is a serial entrepreneur whose journey began in the software realm. His second venture eventually merged into what we now know as PayPal, from which he made a timely exit in 2000 before it was acquired by eBay for a staggering $1.5 billion.

In 2003, Musk launched Tesla, embarking on the ambitious quest to create the first electric car. The Tesla Roadster hit the market in 2008, followed by the Model S sedan in 2012 and the Model X SUV in 2015. Today, Tesla stands as a colossal enterprise valued at over £630 billion, with Musk at the helm, also steering three other ambitious projects: SpaceX, Neuralink, and The Boring Company.

SpaceX represents perhaps Musk's most audacious venture yet. The company is dedicated to developing rockets and spacecraft for missions beyond our atmosphere, with a grand vision of colonising Mars. In 2020, SpaceX made history when its Dragon spacecraft became the first commercial vehicle to transport astronauts to the International Space Station. It also marked the first commercial spacecraft to be successfully recovered after returning from orbit.

Musk is not one to shy away from formidable challenges, and many of his bold decisions have sparked considerable debate. Media outlets have labelled him everything from a "disruptive visionary" to "eccentric" and "erratic." Yet, despite the controversy, he remains one of the wealthiest individuals on the planet, with a fortune nearing £185 billion.

Five Lessons from Elon Musk on Taking Risks

Musk is widely considered a maverick in the world of leadership. Here's what we can learn from him about taking risks.

1. Don't Be Afraid of Failure

"Failure is an option here. If things are not failing, you are not innovating enough," said Musk.

SpaceX has had some very visible, very public failures along the way with three SpaceX rockets exploding before one succeeded. Following this success, an additional three rockets exploded, each holding critical equipment from Facebook and NASA.

But despite the failed launches, critical errors, and exploding rockets, SpaceX flew the Falcon 9 craft to space and back several times and won a $112 million contract from NASA in the process.

Musk is no stranger to failure and even embraces it as part of the process. His mindset — high risk equals high reward.

2. Start Taking Risks Early on in Your Career

"People tend to overrate risk," Musk once said on the subject of entrepreneurship. "It's one thing if you have a mortgage to pay and kids to support… But if you are young and just coming out of college, what do you risk?"

Too often, leaders get caught up worrying about failure. As you advance in your career, that makes sense — you may have a family to support and bigger bills to pay. But taking risks in your younger years can help you to learn and grow.

According to research by Scott Galloway, clinical professor of marketing at NYU's Stern School of Business, most CEOs won't take a risk that has less than a 50% chance of success — no matter how big the potential payoff.

This cautious mindset can prevent companies from growing and innovating. If you're not making mistakes, you aren't taking risks; and if you aren't taking risks, you won't be able to innovate, grow personally and professionally, and create something amazing.

3. Don't Be Afraid of Dumb Ideas

Elon Musk once tweeted, "Creating a rocket company has to be one of the dumbest and hardest ways to 'make money.'" Ironic, coming from one of the world's wealthiest people and the founder of a rocket company.

Nevertheless, Musk's guiding vision is to find solutions for "things that don't seem to be working that are important for our life and the future to be good." That kind of vision requires out-of-the-box thinking, thinking that can sometimes lead to dumb ideas that become less dumb as time goes on.

Dismissing an idea as "dumb" can limit growth and innovation. Dumb ideas often require a lot of hard work and learning to become good ideas, but they can be worth the risk.

4. Take Small Steps Toward Your Big Vision

Musk has said: "When somebody has a breakthrough innovation, it is rarely one little thing. Very rarely, is it one little thing. It's usually a whole bunch of things that collectively amount to a huge innovation."

The path to achieving a big vision is rarely linear. It involves many small steps that bring you closer with each risk you take. SpaceX is a perfect example of this.

"[Musk] was most impressive in cobbling together what was needed for a successful launch site with scraps and whatever was available," said Dale Ketcham, Space Florida vice president of government and external relations, told USA Today. "Some of his most impressive achievements were based on his ability to make stuff happen by using what was available and using simple physics to get done what needed to get done."

Many business leaders hear "risk" and feel anxious. How will you sell a bold new idea to shareholders? Will your newest innovation land with consumers? Start small, build momentum, and figure it out as you go.

5. Risk-taking Is Better Than Playing It Too Safe

True to form, Musk once said, "there's a tremendous bias against taking risks. Everyone is trying to optimise their ass-covering."

More and more business leaders are recognising the value of shifting from a fixed mindset, a belief that things can't be changed, to a growth mindset, believing that your talents and abilities can grow through hard work, good strategies, and support from others. When you shift into that growth mindset, risks become opportunities rather than sources of stress

How to Take Risks Like Elon Musk

What are some ways you can put yourself in the right mindset to take risks? Ask yourself the following questions:

What would make your company, your industry, and our society better in the next 10 years?

At the end of your career, what will you regret NOT doing?

Does your business reward every idea, no matter how bad or dumb?

Is your tolerance for risk impacted by things like student loans, family matters, or other personal circumstances?

Are you challenging your team to think with a growth mindset about the world around you?

Jeff Bezos, Founder of Amazon

We can't celebrate Elon Musk without acknowledging Jeff Bezos, as these two titans of industry are constantly swapping positions as the world's richest entrepreneurs. Amazon began its journey in 1995 as an online bookshop, but how did its visionary founder, Jeff Bezos, manage to transform it into the revolutionary e-commerce powerhouse it is today?

Scaling a business is no small feat. It demands a clear vision, strategic insight, relentless drive, and the courage to make tough, often high-stakes decisions.

You'd be hard-pressed to find anyone who has achieved greater success in scaling a business than Jeff Bezos, the founder and executive chairman of Amazon.

Today, Amazon dominates approximately 40% of the U.S. e-commerce market. One in three Americans holds a Prime membership, and the company rakes in an astonishing £4,722 in sales every single second. In 2020, Amazon reported net sales of £386.06 billion.

Who Is Jeff Bezos?

In July 1994, Wall Street hedge fund executive Jeff Bezos founded Cadabra, which would later become Amazon, from his garage in Bellevue, Washington.

From the very beginning, Bezos was driven by a desire to revolutionise the retail landscape through an online platform, although he was initially uncertain about the company's product range. When Amazon launched its website in July 1995, it specialised solely in books, but the catalogue soon broadened significantly.

Bezos was laser-focused on rapid expansion. By December 1996, Amazon boasted 180,000 registered users, and by October of the following year, that number had surged to approximately one million accounts.

Under Bezos' stewardship, Amazon has acquired numerous companies, including Whole Foods, Audible, and Goodreads. The company has also developed innovative products such as the virtual assistant Alexa and Kindle tablets, alongside launching popular services like Amazon Business and Amazon Web Services.

Today, Bezos' estimated net worth stands at around £200 billion.

5 Lessons on Scaling Your Business from Jeff Bezos

While Jeff Bezos has many commendable leadership traits, not all are viewed positively. Reports suggest that Amazon's work environment can be "notoriously confrontational," and employees have frequently described him as a demanding leader, struggling to retain talent even at the executive level.

Despite his often-challenging demeanour, Bezos's journey in establishing Amazon as a leader in the e-commerce sector offers invaluable insights into scaling a business. Here's how he achieved this remarkable feat.

1. Prioritise the Customer Experience

Though Bezos is known for his rigorous management style, his unwavering focus on customer satisfaction has been paramount.

"The number one thing that has made us successful, by far, is obsessive, compulsive focus on the customer," he stated in a 2018 interview with David Rubenstein.

The introduction of the 1-Click button is a prime example of Amazon's customer-centric innovations. Patented in 1997 and granted in 1999, this feature has generated billions in revenue, allowing customers to make seamless purchases while enabling the company to gather extensive consumer data for tailored marketing.

2. Introduce a Third-party Marketplace

Launched in 2000, Amazon Marketplace revolutionised the platform by allowing third-party vendors to sell their products directly on the site. This move opened a significant revenue stream for Amazon without the complexities of managing inventory.

In 2006, the Fulfilled by Amazon service further enhanced this model, offering to store and ship sellers' products from Amazon's fulfilment centres for a fee, which rapidly expanded the range of offerings available to customers.

3.   Embrace Long-term Vision

Bezos is unafraid to sacrifice short-term profits for long-term gains.

Take, for instance, Amazon's $14 billion acquisition of Whole Foods in 2017, which many viewed as a risky venture. However, Bezos foresaw a growing demand for online grocery ordering and home delivery, a prediction that proved accurate during the surge of food deliveries in 2020-21, especially amid the pandemic.

Another example is Amazon Prime Air. Bezos first mentioned the idea of drone delivery in 2013, investing heavily in its development despite lengthy approval processes. When drone delivery becomes standard, Amazon will reap the benefits of being an early adopter.

4.   Embrace Failure

"If you decide that you're going to do only the things you know are going to work, you're going to leave a lot of opportunity on the table," Bezos remarked.

He firmly believes that success often requires navigating failures. One of Amazon's six core values is a "bias for action," which encourages employees to take risks rather than play it safe.

5. Keep Innovating

Amazon is synonymous with innovation, ranking 11th in U.S. patent filings in 2020. While many of its innovations focus on operational efficiency and tackling challenges, some ideas are intriguingly futuristic, such as:

A whip-based launch system to "snap" objects into orbit.
Flying blimp fulfilment centres.
Underwater warehouses.

Much like fellow billionaire Elon Musk, Bezos's forward-thinking and adventurous spirit led him to enter the space race, founding aerospace manufacturer and suborbital services provider Blue Origin in 2000.

How to Scale Your Business Like Jeff Bezos

Amazon's extraordinary growth has been a sight to behold, and Bezos's strategies for scaling can be applied to businesses of any size.

Consider these questions as you look to grow your own enterprise:

Am I prioritising my customers? How does my product or service enhance their lives, no matter how subtly?

Have I become complacent, or am I actively seeking new growth opportunities?

Am I making decisions with a short-term or long-term perspective?

Am I prepared to take risks that could lead to substantial rewards? Do I encourage my team to take those risks?

Am I allocating time to think creatively and drive innovation in my business?

By reflecting on these points, you can adopt some of the principles that have propelled Jeff Bezos—and Amazon—towards unprecedented success.

Susan Wojcicki, CEO of YouTube.

What Does It Mean to Win the Internet? For many leaders, winning the internet equates to going viral: generating views, clicks, likes, and shares on their content, and ultimately transforming those metrics into sales.

Few understand the art of conquering the online realm better than Susan Wojcicki, one of the most influential women in the world. She has played a pivotal role in some of the internet's most monumental successes.

Wojcicki's career is a treasure trove of insights that can benefit other business leaders eager to make their mark.

Who Is Susan Wojcicki?

Susan Wojcicki served as the CEO of YouTube and boasts over two decades of experience in the tech industry, having started her journey as employee number 16 at Google. During her impressive tenure, she contributed to significant projects like AdSense, Google Analytics, Google Books, and Google Images.

In 2006, Wojcicki proposed that Google acquire YouTube, a bold move that resulted in a purchase for £1.65 billion. Today, YouTube is valued at a staggering £90 billion.

Under her leadership, YouTube has transformed from a platform for amusing cat videos into one of the world's most influential social media channels. Wojcicki spearheaded the development of monetisation strategies for creators, including channel memberships, merchandise sales, and a premium subscription service.

Beyond her achievements in technology, Wojcicki is a passionate advocate for paid family leave and championing gender equality in the tech sector, frequently speaking out against discrimination.

Her career is marked by shrewd investments, from renting her garage to Google founders Sergey Brin and Larry Page during their early days, to acquiring YouTube at what turned out to be a bargain price. Susan Wojcicki truly knows how to win the internet.

5 Lessons on Winning the Internet from Susan Wojcicki

Susan Wojcicki has dedicated considerable time to understanding what content captivates audiences and how to engage them effectively online. From her early days at Google Ads to her role in expanding YouTube, here are five valuable insights that leaders can glean from her journey of internet success.

Content Doesn't Have to Be Perfect to Be Engaging

When Forbes asked Wojcicki about the moment she realised YouTube would be a worthwhile investment, her response highlighted that even the quirkiest content can make a significant impact.

"With YouTube, I remember our first hit was of two Chinese students in their dormitory singing, with their roommate studying in the background. That was the first time I understood that anyone could become a creator and that people were eager to watch content from all sorts of individuals," Wojcicki shared.

As you ponder your own content creation, bear in mind that it doesn't need to be flawless—authenticity and engagement are what truly matter.

Take Time Away from the Digital World

"If you are working non-stop, you're unlikely to generate any innovative ideas," Wojcicki remarked in an interview with the Wall Street Journal in 2016.

Known for her strict policies on turning off emails and limiting phone use both at home and while on holiday, she firmly believes in the importance of being "present." In her experience, regularly unplugging boosts productivity and motivation.

Embrace Failure as a Learning Opportunity

Wojcicki views failure as a stepping stone to growth. "It's essential to confront your mistakes honestly and learn from them," she advised Forbes.

The online landscape can often amplify the sting of failure. However, remember that achieving success on the internet often requires experiencing a fair share of setbacks first. Experiment with various types of content and platforms to discover the best ways to engage your audience and promote yourself effectively.

Be Willing to Pivot When Necessary

Reframing failure as an opportunity can motivate you to make adjustments that lead to greater success. Before Google acquired YouTube, Wojcicki faced challenges with Google's own video product.

"When you realise that a change in strategy is needed or that something isn't working, the instinct may be to resist," she explained. "What you really need to do is embrace it and accept it. The sooner you do, the sooner you can find the right path forward."

This mindset ultimately led to Google's acquisition of YouTube and the discontinuation of its previous video product.

Value and Listen to Feedback

Wojcicki shared the most crucial piece of advice she's received as a leader in the tech industry.

"So often, when people offer feedback, our instinct is to deny it and perceive it as criticism," she noted. "However, I've come to realise that especially as you advance in your career, it's vital to step back, not take it personally, and be open to the feedback."

There's a compelling reason why Wojcicki consistently ranks among the most powerful women in the world. Her ability to listen to feedback and grow as a leader enables her to respond to internet trends with strategic insight and humility.

Other Unmissable Business Leaders Who Changed the World

Let's take a moment to honour some additional leaders whose influence has reshaped the globe.

Lord Alan Sugar

From modest beginnings to a towering icon of success, Lord Alan Sugar embodies the ultimate rags-to-riches tale. His entrepreneurial journey kicked off at a young age, earning pocket money working for a local greengrocer. By just 21, he founded Amstrad, a company that initially sold consumer electronics.

In the 1980s, Amstrad made waves by being listed on the stock exchange, experiencing explosive growth with profits doubling annually. At its pinnacle, the company's stock market value soared to an impressive £1.2 billion. However, Sugar's path wasn't without bumps; the 1990s brought financial setbacks and challenges, including his tumultuous purchase of Tottenham Hotspur Football Club. Yet, he rebounded spectacularly, becoming a household name as the charismatic star of the hit BBC show The Apprentice.

Tim Cook

As the CEO of the world's most valuable company, Apple, Tim Cook stepped into the spotlight following the passing of co-founder Steve Jobs in 2011. Under Cook's guidance, Apple has not only navigated the challenging transition after Jobs' death but has also expanded its product lines and opened new retail stores across China.

Sheryl Sandberg

Sheryl Sandberg served as Chief Operating Officer at Facebook from 2008 to 2022. She founded the nonprofit Lean In, inspired by her best-selling book, and has become a powerful advocate for women in the business arena. Sandberg successfully transitioned from a government role at the Treasury Department to influential positions in the tech industry at Google and Facebook.

Sir Richard Branson

Meet the vibrant, tie-averse founder of the Virgin Group, Sir Richard Branson, whose estimated net worth exceeds a staggering £3 billion, according to Forbes. Much like Lord Sugar, Branson's entrepreneurial spirit ignited early; at just 16, he launched Student, a magazine aimed at young readers. By 20, he ventured into the music industry with a mail-order record business, and soon after, Virgin Records emerged, which would evolve into the iconic Virgin Megastores.

Today, the Virgin brand is everywhere—from Virgin Atlantic to Virgin Trains and Virgin Media—making Branson's wealth no surprise. He's also a familiar face on screen, making cameo appearances in beloved shows like Friends, Only Fools and Horses, and even Baywatch!

Bob Iger

Bob Iger, the Executive Chairman and former CEO of the Disney Corporation, has orchestrated significant acquisitions, including Marvel, Pixar, and Lucas Films. His visionary leadership has also facilitated the expansion of Disney's theme parks into Shanghai and Hong Kong.

Reed Hastings

Reed Hastings is the co-founder and CEO of Netflix. What began as a subscription service with no late fees quickly evolved into a digital streaming powerhouse that transformed the entertainment landscape. Hastings leverages his influence to advocate for reforms in the California State Board of Education and supports charter schools.

Mary Barra

Mary Barra is the Chairman and CEO of General Motors Company. Prior to her current role in 2014, she held the position of Executive Vice President of Global Product Development, Purchasing, and Supply Chain at GM. Barra is making strides in the electric vehicle market, having launched the Chevrolet Bolt EV in 2016, featuring a battery that outlasts Tesla's. In 2017, she was appointed to Disney's board, receiving high praise from Robert Iger.

Huateng "Pony" Ma

Known colloquially as Pony Ma, he is the founder and president of Tencent, one of China's largest internet companies. Recognised twice by Time as one of the world's most influential people (2007 and 2014), Ma is known for his discreet lifestyle while wielding considerable power both domestically and internationally.

Peter Jones

As the longest-serving dragon on the hit BBC show Dragon's Den, Peter Jones has always been a visionary, undeterred by the failures he faced in his 20s. After losing £200,000 on a cocktail bar inspired by the film Cocktail, and facing the downfall of his computer business, he found himself selling his home and cars, moving back in with his parents. But resilience paid off when he launched Phones International Group in 1998; he even slept on the office floor in those early days.

By the end of that first year, revenues skyrocketed to £14 million, marking the beginning of his remarkable comeback. His ongoing success on Dragon's Den solidifies his status as the last remaining original dragon, inspiring countless entrepreneurs along the way.

Jack Ma

Jack Ma made history as the first entrepreneur from mainland China to grace the cover of Forbes magazine. As the founder of Alibaba Group, he overcame numerous rejections in his early life, including being turned down from university three times and receiving no offers after applying for 30 jobs. His journey into the internet world began during a trip to the U.S., leading to the creation of a small website about Chinese products, which eventually paved the way for the largest IPO in history.

Jan Koum

Born in Kyiv, Ukraine, Jan Koum moved to the United States at 16. He soon discovered his passion for programming and enrolled at San José State University. After a brief stint at Yahoo, Koum co-founded WhatsApp, which rapidly became one of the most downloaded apps globally. He sold WhatsApp to Facebook in 2014 for approximately £19.3 billion.

Bill Gates

Bill Gates, the founder of Microsoft, the largest PC software company in the world, is frequently listed among the wealthiest individuals globally. Over the years, he has shifted his focus from Microsoft to philanthropy, with the Bill and Melinda Gates Foundation working to provide clean water and sanitation in developing countries. Like Warren Buffett, Gates has pledged to donate the vast majority of his wealth to charitable causes.

Warren Buffett

Warren Buffett, often referred to as the "Wizard of Omaha," is one of the most successful investors worldwide and consistently ranks among the wealthiest individuals. As CEO of Berkshire Hathaway, he has committed to giving away nearly 99% of his wealth to philanthropic initiatives after his passing.

Jeff Weiner

Jeff Weiner is the CEO of LinkedIn. Although the platform was established in 2002, it was under his leadership that LinkedIn completed its IPO and grew into one of the most-used social media platforms. Weiner is also deeply involved in non-profit work, serving on the Board of Directors for DonorsChoose.org and Malaria No More.

John Zimmer

John Zimmer is the co-founder and president of Lyft, which began in 2012 as Zimride—a rideshare service primarily for college campuses. Since its inception, Zimmer and co-founder Logan Green have transformed Lyft into one of the fastest-growing tech companies.

Ursula Burns

Ursula Burns began her career at Xerox Corporation as a summer intern in 1980 and rose to become the company's president in 2007. She held the chairman position from 2010 to 2017 and was CEO from 2009 to 2016, steering Xerox into one of the world's most diverse business services companies.

Arianna Huffington

In 2005, Arianna Huffington launched The Huffington Post, which quickly became a prominent voice in online journalism. By 2016, she had founded Thrive Global, where she serves as CEO, aiming to transform the way we work and live. Thrive Global has been at the forefront of addressing burnout—essentially coining the term as a professional buzzword long before it gained widespread recognition.

Indra Nooyi

Indra Nooyi held the position of Chairman and CEO at PepsiCo from 2006 to 2019, steering the company with her visionary initiative, Performance with Purpose. This commitment aimed to align business success with the needs of the world, resulting in a greater emphasis on nutritious products, environmental sustainability, and innovative design. Under her leadership, PepsiCo's net revenue soared by over 80%, and shareholders enjoyed an impressive return of 162%.

Meg Whitman

Meg Whitman was at the helm of eBay from 1998 to 2008, propelling the company's sales from £5.7 million to a staggering £8 billion. She later took charge of Hewlett-Packard from 2011 to 2015, managing its significant split into Hewlett Packard Enterprise and HP Inc. Today, she serves as the United States ambassador to Kenya, further extending her influence on the global stage.

Rosalind Brewer

Rosalind Brewer began her career in 2006 with various leadership roles at Walmart, eventually moving to Sam's Club in 2012. Her journey took an exciting turn in 2017 when she became the CEO and Group President of

Starbucks. In 2021, Brewer made headlines as the CEO of Walgreens, marking a historic moment as the first Black woman to lead an S&P 500 company.

Rosalind Brewer

In 2006, Brewer had various leadership positions at Walmart before moving to Sam's Club in 2012. Her tenure at Sam's Club ended in 2017 when she moved to become the CEO and Group President of Starbucks. In 2021, she became CEO of Walgreens, making her a particularly famous business leader as she is the only Black woman CEO for an S&P 500 company.

X HOW TO BECOME A RADIATOR

"A strong positive mental attitude will create more miracles than any wonder drug" - Patricia Neal

You need PMA in your life – Positive Mental Attitude

I f there's one thing that we've learnt writing this book, it's that radiators take many forms and personalities, but they all have one thing in common, the have a deep inherent Positive Mental Attitude. It is probably not a surprise to you that PMA is, inherently, at the centre of positive psychology.

Positivity doesn't always refer to simply smiling and looking cheerful; positivity is more about one's overall perspective on life and your tendency to focus on all that is good in life and business.

In this chapter, we'll cover the basics of positivity from a psychological perspective, identify some of the many benefits of approaching life from a positive point of view, and explore some tips and techniques for cultivating a positive mindset.

What is PMA? A Definition

You may already have some understanding of what a positive mindset or attitude entails, but it's always beneficial to start with a clear definition.

Remez Sasson offers a succinct description:

"Positive thinking is a mental and emotional attitude that focuses on the bright side of life and anticipates positive outcomes."

For a more in-depth perspective, Kendra Cherry from Very Well Mind provides a richer definition:

"Positive thinking means tackling life's challenges with an optimistic outlook. It doesn't imply that we should ignore the negatives; rather, it encourages us to navigate potentially adverse situations, seek the best in others, and view ourselves and our abilities in a favourable light."

From these insights, we can distil a positive mindset into the tendency to shine a light on the brighter side, expect uplifting results, and face challenges with an optimistic approach.

Embracing a positive mindset involves cultivating the habit of positive thinking, consistently looking for the silver linings, and striving to make the most of every situation you encounter.

Characteristics and Traits of a Positive Mindset: 6 Engaging Examples

Now that we've established what a positive mindset entails, let's explore the next vital question: What does it actually look like in practice?

A positive mindset is marked by several key traits and characteristics, including:

- Optimism: This is the courage to make an effort and take a leap of faith, rather than assuming your endeavours will lead to disappointment.

- Acceptance: It's about recognising that things won't always unfold as you wish, but instead of dwelling on setbacks, you learn and grow from them.

- Resilience: This trait empowers you to bounce back from challenges, disappointments, and failures rather than succumbing to defeat.

- Gratitude: This involves a continuous appreciation for the good in your life, fostering a sense of contentment and joy.

- Mindfulness: This is the practice of being fully aware and present, sharpening your focus and enhancing your mental clarity.

- Integrity: Being honourable, principled, and straightforward, rather than deceitful or self-serving, is a hallmark of this characteristic.

These traits not only define a positive mindset but can also reinforce each other—actively embracing optimism, acceptance, resilience, gratitude, mindfulness, and integrity in your daily life will significantly help you cultivate and sustain a positive outlook.

Our List of Positive Attitudes

If the previous list felt a bit too abstract, let's delve into some more specific examples of a positive attitude in action in the real world. The theory of PMA can be hard to implement but we can all recognise the characteristics that radiators adopt that we admire.

So, we've identified behaviours that we can all emulate, embracing positivity in the workplace and in our everyday life, and ultimately asking the question, what would a radiator do:

WTF moments: Facing challenges head-on… and having a good chuckle about it. Laughing at the absurdity of some situations and actively using humour to deflect and rephrase is a good way to reduce the impact and avoid stress. Sharing with like-minded friends who use humour in similar ways is a common way to defuse a potentially stressful journey.

Whatever! Accepting what life throws your way without throwing a tantrum is crucial. Many radiators find joy in the unexpected, even when it's not quite what they had in mind. When you are so confident in finding a solution or some positivity in the face of adversity that you can simply shrug it off, this is empowering.

Smile tactics: Harnessing the power of a smile to change the mood of a situation works of two levels. Firstly, smiling induces more pleasure in the brain more than chocolate. I know you might not believe this but according to Ron Gutman, the author of *Smile: The Astonishing Powers of a Simple Act*, British researchers found that one smile can generate the same level of brain stimulation as up to 2,000 bars of chocolate.

Secondly, a smile can throw your adversary off track. Drains thrive off the pain and discomfort they create and so a simple smile shows you're not affected by their tactics and that you are in control. Try it but avoid the smirk.

Get back on the horse: Picking yourself up after a fall, no matter how many times it happens, is a crucial quality for radiators. Metaphorically speaking, the quicker you can respond to a blow, the less time you have to wallow in the pain you've received.

The phrase "get back on the horse" means to try something again after failing. It comes from the idea that if you fall off a horse while riding, you should climb back on and keep trying. This idiom encourages people not to give up, even if they face setbacks.

No complaints: It's easy to assume that the high standards that business leaders radiate, means that they are always complaining. The opposite is in fact true, no matter how unfair things may seem, radiators never waste their energy complaining believing it far better to take action!

Constant complaining causes real damage. It's like a bad habit that physically alters your brain over time. The more you complain, the more habitual it becomes and the more it rewires your brain. Neuroscientists have found that the connections between the neurons in our brains that fire together repeatedly become stronger. So, the more you repeat a behaviour, like complaining, the more strongly connected those neurons become. Over time, this "strengthening" process forms a neural pathway in the brain that makes that behaviour a habit.

Finding a suitable action to improve a situation is far healthier than complaining about it.

Happy problem solving: Enjoying yourself, even when things aren't going your way, is an art. This is because, in most cases, the problem is not the problem but how you perceive it.

As humans, we have a habit to associate things not going our way as being a problem. But more often than not, those problems are not really what they first seem. The reason we view them as problems is that they are different from the outcome we expected. In other words, they are merely circumstances that bring about temporary discomfort. But one can never grow from a place of comfort, it is always through the trying times that we learn to figure out the next step we must take. So, when things are going your way, it's time for a new path that leads to personal growth.

Celebrate others success: Telling someone you know that they did a fantastic job—and meaning it, feels great. You're not only brightening someone's day, you are filling your own self-esteem bucket. This is what radiators do naturally so let's embrace this habit.

Stay true to yourself: Being true to yourself sounds simple, but it's often harder than it seems. Every day, we face choices. Some big, like choosing a career, and some small, like deciding what to wear. Yet, each decision tells us a bit about who we are.

How do you stay true to who you are in a world full of so many different voices and opinions? To live a life that genuinely reflects your values and desires, you must know yourself and have the courage to follow that knowledge wherever it may lead. This means listening to your heart and being honest with yourself. It's knowing your likes and dislikes and understanding your deep motivations. Your core values are like your personal rulebook. They shape your decisions and actions, basically shaping your life based on what matters most to you.

Listen to Your Inner Voice: Deep within you lies a small companion brimming with wise advice—your inner voice. It's a treasure trove of insights that deserves your attention as you navigate the journey to becoming your authentic self.

In the hustle and bustle of life, it's easy to drown out that gentle wisdom. So, take a moment to pause. A few deep breaths and a bit of stillness can help your inner voice finally speak up.

This voice may encourage you to decline a job offer that doesn't excite you or to take a bold step towards a long-held dream. The more you tune in, the clearer its guidance becomes. Listening to your inner voice can steer you away from choices that don't resonate and help you feel more confident in those that do. It's remarkable how it directs you exactly where you need to go.

Honour Your Feelings: Your feelings are integral to who you are, making it crucial to heed their messages. When something feels off or when joy bubbles up, consider it a signal—your intuition is communicating with you. Sometimes, societal pressures may tempt you to suppress your true feelings to maintain harmony or due to concerns about others' opinions. Resist that urge.

Honouring your feelings means recognising them as valid, even if you don't act on them immediately. This practice fosters deeper self-understanding and allows you to make choices that genuinely reflect your needs and aspirations. Grant yourself permission to experience whatever emotions arise. There's no need for harsh self-judgment. By respecting your feelings, you're more likely to make decisions that align with your true self.

Appreciate the Person in the Mirror: When was the last time you paused, looked into the mirror, and genuinely smiled at the person before you? That individual, with all their delightful imperfections, is you—and they deserve your appreciation.

It's all too easy to be your own harshest critic, focusing solely on what you wish to change. However, embracing your true self begins with appreciating who you see in the mirror. Acknowledge your smile, your resilience in tough situations, or simply your ability to rise when the alarm sounds.

Stop Comparing Yourself to Others: We call it the Facebook Syndrome, it's all too simple to glance at someone else's life and think they've got it all figured out. But here's the truth—each of us follows a distinct path, facing unique challenges and celebrating different victories. If you're constantly measuring your life against others, you're setting yourself up for disappointment. Instead, concentrate on your own journey. Reflect on how far you've come and the obstacles you've overcome. Your path is uniquely yours, with its own exciting twists and turns—celebrate your achievements, no matter how small.

Lastly, when you find yourself slipping into the comparison trap, remind yourself that the only person you need to surpass is the one you were yesterday. By doing so, you grant yourself the freedom to pursue your own journey at your own pace.

When we compare ourselves, we automatically place ourselves in second place. Why? Because we can never be that person. We can never live their life, share their experiences, or have their body. We were never meant to be them; we were born to be ourselves. By comparing ourselves, we diminish our own worth, whereas if we stopped comparing, we would always come out on top.

Speak *Your* Truth: Expressing your true thoughts can sometimes feel challenging, but it's absolutely essential. Your ideas and opinions matter, and they deserve to be heard. Begin by clarifying what you truly believe. If there's something you're passionate about, don't hesitate to share it. When you're open about your feelings and thoughts, you reveal your authentic self to the world.

If being forthright isn't your usual style, start with small, low-stakes situations. For instance, rather than simply agreeing to a plan that doesn't resonate with you, propose an alternative. This practice will gradually bolster your confidence, allowing you to articulate deeper feelings and opinions when it counts.

There's no need to be aggressive or impolite. You can be both honest and kind. If you find yourself at odds with someone, it's possible to express your disagreement respectfully. This isn't about persuading others to see things your way; it's about embracing your true self without fear.

Do What Is Best for You: Choosing what's best for yourself may seem straightforward, but it often involves a deep understanding of who you are and sometimes making difficult decisions. This means considering what genuinely matters to you: your health, your aspirations, and your happiness.

Here's 3 simple steps to embark on this journey:

- Reflect on decisions through the lens of your well-being.
- Trust your instincts; you know what's best for you.
- Remember, prioritising your own needs isn't selfish.

When you start making choices that align with your best interests, it's like taking the helm of your own life. Not everyone will grasp your decisions, and that's perfectly fine. You've got this!

Check In With Yourself: Checking in with yourself is akin to giving your mind and heart a moment to pause and reconnect. It can help you remain centred and make choices that resonate with who you are.

Here's how best to do it:

- Carve out quiet time: Even if it's just five minutes a day, find a tranquil space to reflect on your thoughts.
- Pose essential questions: How am I feeling today? What brings me joy or discontent? Is there something I need that I'm currently missing?
- Document your reflections: Keeping a journal can be a valuable tool for tracking your thoughts and feelings over time, aiding your personal growth journey.

This daily self-check is a simple yet powerful way to stay attuned to your needs. It's an opportunity to recognise when you might need a break, some enjoyment, or simply a good night's sleep. By checking in with yourself, you're prioritising your well-being and ensuring you remain true to your desires and aspirations in life.

Make Time for Reflection: Every now and then, it's a good idea to hit pause and think about where you're at in life. It's like checking your own roadmap to make sure you're still on the path you want to be on. Make it a part of your routine. Start by setting aside at least 10 minutes each day. Choose a time that suits you best, maybe in the evening when things have quieted down, and keep it consistent. Put it in your daily dairy and treat this as a mini-appointment with yourself.

In your reflection time, focus on three specific areas:

1. Actions: What did you do today? Maybe you helped a friend in need or tackled a tough project at work.
2. Reactions: How did you respond to challenges? Were you patient in the long queue at the store, or did you let frustration get the best of you?
3. Intentions: Did you live today the way you wanted to? Perhaps you intended to eat healthy but ended up having fast food for lunch.

This simple exercise does wonders for keeping you in line with your core values and goals. It's not about beating yourself up for the things that didn't go well. Instead, the aim is to recognise what you can learn from each day.

The most important requirement to find one's true nature is self-awareness. We grew up being influenced by what family members, teachers, booses and friends told us who we should be, and what we should and should not do. We bought into their stories.

By asking ourselves, "Who am I?" "How do I feel?" "What do I desire?" and "What is my purpose in life?" we bring awareness to our inner voice. The more we hone it, the better it will guide us...

Only then will we be able to break away from other people's stories, stop living to please others, and get rid of what is no longer working for us. Slowly, our true self will emerge, and our inner voice will provide us with the knowingness of what is best for us, and we become authors of our own story."

Embrace Time Alone: Learning to be comfortable in your own company is a valuable skill for everyone. When you find yourself alone, you create the perfect opportunity to think clearly and reflect without outside influences clouding your thoughts.

Being at ease with solitude means engaging in activities you might typically share with others. Treat yourself to a trip to the cinema, explore a museum, or enjoy a meal at a restaurant on your own. Initially, it might feel a bit odd, but many discover that these solo excursions are both refreshing and empowering. It's a powerful affirmation that you can have fun all on your own.

This time spent alone provides a wonderful chance to reconnect with your passions and desires, free from external opinions. It fosters a deeper sense of independence and confidence in your choices—essential elements of living authentically.

Be Mindful with Your Time: To live an authentic life, it's crucial to use your time wisely. This means making deliberate choices about how you spend your days, ensuring that your activities align with your personal values and aspirations. Here's a simple approach:

- Prioritise Tasks: Begin by identifying what's most important for your personal and professional goals. Anything that doesn't support these priorities may not warrant your attention right now.

- Set Boundaries: Decide how much time to allocate to each activity. This helps prevent overcommitting and maintains a healthy balance in your life.

- Learn to Say No: Part of being mindful is having the courage to decline opportunities that don't align with your priorities. While it can be challenging, saying no opens the door to what truly matters. *Saying No is important, so there's more on this later in this chapter.*

Being mindful doesn't mean you need to fill every moment with activity. Sometimes, it's about recognising when you need a break. This not only helps prevent burnout but also keeps your mind sharp and aligned with your journey towards authenticity.

Pursue Your Passions: Chasing after the things you love makes life infinitely richer, doesn't it? Whether it's painting, hiking, or coding, carve out time for your passions. Even amidst a busy schedule, you can often find a few hours each week for what truly makes your heart sing.

One practical step is to set specific goals related to your interests. For instance, if writing is your passion, aim to craft a page each day or submit a story to a magazine monthly. These small steps keep you connected to what you adore and significantly enhance your sense of self.

Pursuing your passions is like unwrapping a gift for yourself. It reminds you of what brings you joy beyond your roles and responsibilities. Plus, it's a fantastic way to meet others who share your enthusiasm!

Prioritise Self-Care: Treat yourself with the same kindness you'd extend to a cherished friend. Self-care is essential for helping you thrive, both mentally and physically. It goes beyond indulgent spa days or occasional treats; it's about making consistent, healthy choices that nurture your overall well-being.

Here's how to seamlessly integrate self-care into your daily routine:

- Get Plenty of Sleep – A good night's rest is a game-changer.
- Stay Active – Whether it's dancing, jogging, or simply stretching, your body will thank you for moving.
- Don't Skip Meals – Your brain needs proper fuel to tackle the day ahead.

Remember, when you prioritise your self-care, you show up as a stronger, happier version of yourself, ready to take on whatever comes your way.

Observe Yourself: This needs to be both alone and in the company of friends. Taking note of how you behave when you're on your own versus in a social setting can reveal much about your values and feelings. When you're by yourself, pay attention to the activities you gravitate toward without outside influence. Do you choose to read, scribble, or play music? These choices reflect your true interests. When you're with friends, observe how you might alter your behaviour. Do you hold back your opinions or go along with the crowd even when you disagree? This awareness can help you pinpoint areas where you might not be fully authentic or where peer pressure may be swaying your decisions.

The aim here isn't self-judgement but rather increased awareness. Recognising these patterns is the first step toward making choices that align more closely with your personal values and aspirations.

Never Settle for Less Than You Truly Desire: It's all too easy to accept less than what you truly want, especially when it feels convenient. However, settling can lead to dissatisfaction and regret in the long run. To live a life that reflects your true self, it's crucial to strive for what genuinely brings you happiness and fulfilment.

Start by taking some time to reflect on what you truly desire in various aspects of your life, such as your career, personal relationships, and hobbies. What does your ideal situation look like? Jot down your thoughts to clarify your vision and create a reference point. Once you have a clear idea of what you want, devise a plan to achieve it. This might involve setting specific goals, acquiring new skills, or changing your environment. The key is to take consistent actions that guide you toward your ideal outcomes.

Staying true to your desires may require making some tough choices, like leaving a comfortable job or ending a stable relationship that doesn't fulfil you. Remember, each step you take toward what you genuinely want is a step toward a more authentic life. Embrace those steps with confidence.

Master the Art of Saying No: Navigating the delicate dance of saying 'no' can be quite a challenge, especially when you're keen to avoid disappointing others. However, remember, it's your time and your life—you're the one in control. When you agree to things you're not genuinely interested in, you're inadvertently saying 'no' to opportunities that may hold far more significance for you.

Here's how to refine your 'no' skills:

- Pause Before You Reply: You're not obliged to respond with a 'yes' or 'no' immediately. Take your time.
- Be Clear Yet Kind: There's no need for elaborate explanations. A straightforward refusal can be delivered with warmth.
- Realise the Value of Every 'No': Each time you say 'no', you're creating space for a 'yes' to something that truly resonates with you.

The more you practice this, the easier it will become. Before long, you'll find you have more time for the pursuits that genuinely excite you. Plus, when others see you valuing your own time, they'll begin to do the same.

Stop Being a People Pleaser: Breaking free from the habit of trying to please everyone is a significant leap towards embracing your authentic self. It's crucial to recognise that it's impossible to satisfy everyone without sacrificing pieces of your own identity.

If you're constantly bending over backwards for others, you may forget how to stand tall for yourself. So, take a moment to reflect—are you agreeing to things out of genuine desire, or simply to avoid causing a stir? Start small by checking in with your feelings before you automatically say yes. If your instincts whisper, "I'm not really up for this," heed that voice! It's perfectly acceptable to prioritise your own preferences from time to time. Your honesty may be just what others need, and they'll begin to appreciate the real you.

Once you do this, you'll feel a sense of relief, and who knows—you might even find more joy in activities that truly make you happy.

Establish Boundaries with Others: Setting clear boundaries is essential in defining how you wish to be treated and what behaviours you find acceptable. It's about respecting yourself enough to say, "This is where I draw the line."

Here's how to get started:

- Define Your Limits: Understand what you're comfortable with and communicate that to others. For instance, if you prefer not to be contacted about work during weekends, make that known to your colleagues.
- Communicate Openly and Kindly: When establishing boundaries, honesty is key, but so is

kindness. A simple phrase like, "I cherish our time together, but I need weekends to recharge," sets clear expectations without causing offence.

- Enforce Your Boundaries: It's one thing to set boundaries; it's another to uphold them. Don't hesitate to remind others when they're crossing the line. Consistency is vital for ensuring that your limits are respected.

Setting boundaries is akin to erecting a protective fence that keeps the positive in and the stress out. Those people worth having in your life will respect your boundaries and likely appreciate you all the more for setting them.

Walk Away from What No Longer Serves You: Life is too precious to cling to things that don't bring you joy or help you grow. Perhaps it's a job that feels stagnant, or a hobby that no longer sparks your enthusiasm. Start by reflecting on what drains your energy or consumes your time without providing any real reward. If something feels more exhausting than fulfilling, it might be time to reconsider your commitment to it. You could begin by reducing the time you spend on these activities instead of making a sudden exit.

Letting go can be challenging, especially if something has been a significant part of your life for a while. However, remember that prioritising your own well-being is perfectly acceptable. By stepping away from what no longer serves you, you create room for better opportunities that align more closely with who you are today.

Final Thoughts: Remaining true to yourself is a daily commitment. Each day brings fresh challenges and choices that test our honesty and bravery. The journey may not always be straightforward, but embracing your true self is worth every step along the way. Remember, each time you choose authenticity, you're putting yourself first.

As we conclude, consider the small steps you can take each day to be more genuine in your actions and decisions. Listen to your heart, trust your instincts, and stand firm in who you are. The more you practise this, the more effortless it becomes.

XI HELP... I THINK I'M A DRAIN

*None knows the weight
of another's burden -
George Herbert*

Feel Like a Burden to Others? Why and What to Do

The famous quote by George Herbert is a reminder that we cannot really comprehend the struggles of another individual. We might assume we understand what they are going through, their own personal struggles or what they are experiencing, but the reality is we can never absolutely recognise the weight of their burden. Everybody has their own one-of-a-kind struggles, and the quote urges us to be compassionate and resist evaluating based upon our very own experiences. It advises us that everyone is going through something, and we should be mindful of that.

Feeling like a burden can significantly disrupt our lives, preventing us from opening up about our struggles with those who care. It can also hinder us from forming close connections in the first place. If you find yourself feeling like a drain on others, you might notice some tell-tale signs: feeling guilty when you seek help, experiencing anxiety or guilt when discussing your problems, or believing that others only spend time with you out of obligation rather than genuine enjoyment.

By understanding the reasons behind these feelings and adopting some helpful strategies, you can begin to feel less like a burden. This, in turn, paves the way for deeper, more fulfilling relationships and a greater sense of self-worth.

How to stop feeling like a drain

Feeling like a real drain is something you can learn to overcome. A lot of the battle is learning to have self-compassion and prioritise self-care. Recognising situations where these thoughts come up and learning to challenge and reframe the thoughts into healthier ones can also be quite helpful. We've compiled some easy steps that can put you on the path to positivity:

1. **Challenge the thoughts you have about yourself**

Notice when you're feeling like a burden and learn to let it go without letting those feelings control you.

Imagine you need to ask a friend or colleague for assistance, and suddenly, you feel a wave of self-doubt washing over you. Thoughts like, "I should be able to sort this out myself," or "They've got enough on their plate already," might spring to mind.

This is your cue to challenge those thoughts! Remind yourself, "Ah, there's that 'I'm a drain' narrative rearing its head again! Just because I feel like a burden doesn't mean I truly am one. People appreciate me, and they want to help. I deserve support just like anyone else."

Reframing your thoughts in this way can diminish their hold over you.

2. **Boost Your Self-Esteem**

A fantastic way to enhance your self-esteem is to set small, achievable goals and allow yourself to bask in the pride of accomplishing them.

Keep your goals manageable and realistic. The key is to clearly define what you want to achieve, ensuring it doesn't require too much time or effort initially. Celebrate each small victory along the way! Take, for instance, the phrase "I want to get fit." It's a bit vague, isn't it? Instead, why not commit to taking the stairs instead of the lift for two flights on your way to work, just once a day?

You might also consider setting small, achievable goals like journaling before bed or first thing in the morning, meditating for just two minutes daily, or making it a habit to floss every night when you brush your teeth. The key is to tailor your goals to your current circumstances and remain realistic. Once you feel at ease with your new routine, don't hesitate to build on it. And remember to celebrate your progress! Acknowledge the positive changes you're making in your life.

3. **Open Up About Your Feelings**

Often, merely sharing what you're feeling with someone else can lighten the load, even if they can't offer advice or solutions. This is why many support groups encourage a rule of "no cross-talk." When someone shares, the others simply listen without providing feedback or counsel. As you work on enhancing your social life, consider joining support groups—either online or in person—as well as exploring online forums.

Platforms like Mind, NSHN forum, and Sane are dedicated to various forms of support and can be excellent spaces to vent and seek help when you feel like a burden to those around you.

4. Reframe Your Apologies

Do you find yourself perpetually saying sorry? If you're constantly apologising for everything, you might start to feel like you need to apologise for simply existing. The language we use shapes our reality.

Instead of saying, "I'm sorry for going on so much," try saying, "Thank you for listening." This small shift can leave both you and your conversation partner feeling more empowered.

5. Remember, Others Feel the Same

Many people experience feelings of being a burden at some point in their lives. If we live long enough, we all encounter challenges we worry might be "too much" for others—be it divorce, health issues, mental health struggles, unhealthy relationships, financial troubles, career setbacks, and so on.

For instance, a survey of terminally ill patients revealed that 39.1% reported feeling like a burden as a minimal or mild concern, while 38% indicated it as a moderate to extreme worry.

6. Examine Your Feelings About Your Loved Ones

When a loved one approaches you with their problems, do you perceive them as a burden? How do you respond to them in their times of struggle? We sometimes feel like we don't have the emotional bandwidth to deal with other people's problems when we're overwhelmed with life ourselves, but we still tend to view the people we care about in a positive light.

Instead of seeing them as a "drain" or something we need to "deal with," we can see that they're struggling and feel empathy and care towards them. Likewise, the people who care about you will think positively of you even when you feel like you're "too much." Try to believe that they care about you and appreciate having you in their life, even when you can't feel it.

7. Improve your relationships

If your friends or romantic partner actively contributes to you feeling like a burden, it's time to take some serious steps to improve the relationship.

It can be hard to separate whether the issue is ours (we take their words too seriously due to our insecurity) or theirs (they are being insensitive or even cruel).

Often in relationships, it is not the case that one side is always wrong, and the other person is always right.

If your partner is making you feel like a burden and they are not open to couple's therapy, there are still steps you can take by yourself to improve your relationship. Work to understand how you can improve your communication, learn to set boundaries, and healthily express your needs.

By improving your relationship skills, the relationships around you will naturally start to improve. You'll also get better at recognising which relationships no longer serve you and feel more comfortable walking away from people who make you feel bad and aren't willing to do the work to create a relationship that works for the both of you.

Reasons why you may feel like a drain

We often take our thoughts and feelings as fact. We assume that if we feel like we're a burden to those around us, that means that there is something inside us that is flawed and that we need to fix. The reality is that there are several common reasons why individuals may come to believe they are a burden to those around them. By understanding these reasons, you can address the issues head-on.

1. Depression and Mood Disorders

Depression can significantly alter our perception of the world, often leading to the painful belief that we are a burden. This feeling can drive those suffering from depression into isolation, which only exacerbates their condition.

Depression brings with it a heavy weight of emotions—loneliness, despair, hopelessness, irritability, anger, and even thoughts of self-harm. Those experiencing depression often find that the joy they once derived from activities fades away. Consequently, they may fear that sharing their feelings will only "bring others down" or that those around them won't understand and will feel worse as a result. A person might think, "Everyone would be better off without me, as I'm just useless and miserable all the time."

2. Anxiety Disorders

Anxiety often centres on specific triggers—be it exams, health concerns, or accidents—but generalised anxiety and social anxiety are also prevalent. Such feelings can lead to the worry that others will react negatively if you open up about your struggles.

Even when someone with anxiety realises that their thoughts may not be entirely rational, those thoughts can still wield a profound influence over their life. Often, anxiety can spiral; for instance, if someone feels anxious about making phone calls, they might start to avoid them altogether. This avoidance can give rise to further anxieties, such as worrying that "No one will want to be friends with me if I can't return their calls."

Supportive friends and family may step in to help with anxiety-inducing tasks (like making calls on your behalf), but the anxious individual may still feel guilt for relying on others.

3. Low Self-Esteem

Low self-esteem can be linked to depression, anxiety, and difficult childhood experiences, but it can also exist in its own right. When you struggle with low self-worth, it's easy to convince yourself that you're less important than those around you. This can lead to feelings of being a burden when you share your experiences or "take up space" in any way. You might feel that your personality or presence is an inconvenience to others and may even question the authenticity of your friendships.

4. Feeling Like a Burden in Childhood

Regrettably, many of us grew up with parents who struggled to meet our emotional needs. Instead of seeking to understand our feelings when we cried, they might have simply tried to silence us. If we expressed anger, they could react with frustration rather than empathy, leading us to suppress our emotions.

In some instances, parents were absent due to divorce, mental health issues, long work hours, or other circumstances. Even when they were present, they might have been distracted, irritable, or overwhelmed, leaving us feeling emotionally neglected. At times, parents may have seemed more focused on our achievements than on our emotional well-being. Additionally, some children bear the weight of significant responsibilities, such as caring for younger siblings or managing household tasks, further instilling a sense of being a burden. This type of upbringing is called childhood emotional neglect, and one common symptom is feeling like we are deeply flawed inside or a burden to others. Feeling like a burden to our parents early on becomes embedded in our belief system, even if we don't have specific memories of feeling like a burden, and even if our parents could meet our physical needs.

In some cases, emotional neglect from childhood can lead to Complex-PTSD. In these situations, professional help is often the only answer.

5. Navigating Challenging Life Situations

At times, we can find ourselves lagging behind our peers in significant ways. Perhaps your friends and acquaintances are advancing in their careers, enjoying lucrative salaries, while you feel trapped in a dead-end job with meagre pay.

Maybe a friend occasionally treats you, leaving you with a sense of guilt. Or they might suggest a holiday together, but it's out of your financial reach, while their other friends can easily join in. In such scenarios, it's easy to feel like a financial burden, unable to partake in outings the way your friends can.

You might also be facing a disability or grappling with serious physical or mental health challenges, which can leave your partner shouldering most of the household responsibilities. These situations are undeniably tough, as there's a stark reality that's hard to overlook.

6. Feeling Like a Burden in Your Relationships

There are times when we find ourselves in relationships where our partner struggles to meet our emotional needs. Your husband, wife, boyfriend, or girlfriend may, whether deliberately or inadvertently, make you feel like a burden.

If your partner dismisses your feelings when you open up about your struggles or expresses frustration at having to support you, it's entirely natural to start feeling like you're weighing them down.

Tips for Business and Life:

Managing feelings of being a drain can be challenging, both in business and our personal lives. We've explored many strategies in this chapter, but here are some brief tips to help navigate these emotions:

In Business:

Foster Open Communication: Create a culture where team members feel safe discussing challenges. Encourage regular check-ins to openly address concerns.

Seek Feedback: Regularly ask for feedback from colleagues or supervisors. This can help you gain perspective and reassurance, reducing feelings of inadequacy.

Set Realistic Expectations: Avoid overcommitting. Understand your limits and communicate them clearly to your team, ensuring everyone is on the same page

Build a Supportive Network: Cultivate relationships with colleagues who understand your experiences. Having a support system can help you feel less isolated.

Focus on Strengths: Concentrate on your strengths and contributions to the team. Recognising your value can counteract feelings of being a burden.

Encourage Team Collaboration: Promote teamwork and collaboration, where everyone contributes and supports one another. This can help create a sense of belonging and reduce individual feelings of inadequacy.

In Life:

Acknowledge Your Feelings: Recognise that feeling like a burden is a common experience. It's okay to have these feelings and acknowledging them is the first step toward addressing them.

Communicate Openly: Talk to trusted friends or family members about how you feel. Sharing your thoughts can help alleviate the burden and foster deeper connections.

Practice Self-Compassion: Treat yourself with the same kindness you would offer a friend. Remind yourself that everyone has struggles, and it's okay to seek support.

Reframe Your Thoughts: Challenge negative thoughts by reframing them. Instead of thinking, "I'm a burden," try "I'm human, and it's okay to ask for help."

Seek Professional Help: If feelings of being a burden persist, consider talking to a therapist or counsellor. They can provide strategies to cope and improve your self-esteem.

Engage in Self-Care: Prioritise activities that nurture your well-being, whether it's exercise, hobbies, or relaxation techniques. Caring for yourself can boost your mood and reduce feelings of burden.

By implementing these strategies, you can navigate feelings of being a burden more effectively, allowing for healthier relationships in both personal and professional settings.

XII RADIATE - THE PHYSCOLOGY OF SELLING

When we keep claiming the light, we will find ourselves becoming more and more radiant - Henri Nouwen

The Psychology Behind Sales

Salespeople play a crucial role in driving our economy forward. They are the heartbeat of businesses, generating the revenue that fuels the creation of the products and services we rely on every day. This, in turn, supports the salaries that empower consumers to make purchases, creating a vibrant cycle of commerce. Moreover, businesses contribute taxes that fund essential government services, from education and healthcare to social security. Without the engine of sales, our society would face serious challenges, it might even collapse.

Those who excel in sales often enjoy substantial incomes and a strong sense of job security. However, while many embark on this career path, only a select few achieve remarkable success, leading to a stark contrast between the top performers and those who struggle. In fact, according to a 2018 Salesforce survey, well over half (57%) of all salespeople fail to even hit their base targets. So why do so many of us as salespeople fall short of our potential?

To uncover the secrets of success in sales, we delve into the psychology of top performers, exploring what drives their achievements, while also examining the mindsets of customers and clients who become the buyers and discover what really happens in the buyer-seller dance.

Are you really radiating?

You've delved deep into Drains & Radiators, and you're well aware of the importance of maintaining a positive outlook. You've done your research, and you know your product inside out—you're ready to sell! Your passion for what you offer shines through, leading you to believe you're a standout seller. Yet, the hard truth is, from the buyer's perspective, your approach might not be hitting the mark.

Even the most optimistic sellers often fall back on their "people skills," trying to adapt their pitch and manage the sales interaction. Unfortunately, this approach typically backfires, leaving them feeling overshadowed by the buyer, desperately pursuing the sale, and willing to do almost anything to close the deal. There's a common misconception that high-pressure tactics are the secret to achieving and exceeding sales targets—but that's simply not the case.

This amateur strategy hands over control to the buyer, placing the salesperson in a reactive position where the pressure mounts. The responsibility lies solely with the buyer, creating tension that drains energy from both sides. Does this sound familiar?

Back in the mid-1970s, David H. Sandler recognised the urgent need for a better way to sell. Frustrated by the outdated, high-pressure methods employed by many novice salespeople, he set out to find a more effective approach. Sandler's journey went beyond merely developing new sales techniques. He thoroughly re-evaluated sales processes and strategies, scrutinising his own behaviours in the process. He even sought insights from clinical psychologists regarding the attitudes and belief systems of both buyers and sellers. Drawing from this extensive research, Sandler gradually crafted a robust professional sales methodology that integrated innovative business communication principles— well ahead of its time.

Today, his effective and efficient sales process is taught in over 25 countries and 15 languages. Those who embrace it often describe it as a game changer, demonstrating how to work smarter, sell more, and do so with greater efficiency.

Sandler recognised that in what he termed the "buyer-seller dance," two distinct systems are always at play: the buyer's system and the salesperson's system. To take the lead in this intricate process, you must master the dance, which involves understanding and applying an effective selling methodology. Simply turning up at the sales meeting, offering assistance, and educating your buyer is simply not sufficient. This is when the radiant salesperson actually, in the eyes of the buyer, becomes a drain.

Ideally, the sales process should be perceived as a win-win scenario. However, any salesperson who has spent time in the field knows that buyers often view themselves as individuals with something to protect: their money, time, and reputation. Consequently, they tend to adopt a confrontational stance towards salespeople.

Many salespeople admit they are unaware of the manipulative tactic's buyers may employ during sales calls. This lack of awareness often leads to failure, as they struggle to take control of the selling process and guide buyers through it as trusted consultants. Contrary to common belief, selling is a commendable profession, and the sales process can be an enjoyable experience for both parties. Assisting others through your sales journey is a genuine, tangible, and teachable skill.

Salespeople truly have the ability to eliminate uncertainty, anxiety, and pressure from the sales process—provided they grasp the psychology behind the sale and understand what makes an opportunity worth pursuing. They should be aware of their position within the sales process and have a clear idea of what comes next.

Sandler developed his own sales methodology 'the Sandler Way' based on these fundamental principles:

- Salespeople are professionals and deserve respect.
- It is the buyer who must qualify for the salesperson's time, not the other way around.
- Salespeople should adhere to a repeatable and scalable system.

What we truly need is a transformative sales methodology that revolutionises the approach to selling. One that empowers you to work smarter, increase your sales, and enhance efficiency.

You may not secure every sale, but at least you'll have a clear understanding of each sales call. More importantly, you'll know precisely how to respond!

Often, inexperienced salespeople lack awareness of what's unfolding during a sales call because they allow the buyer to take the lead. Let's delve deeper into how and why the buyer's system proves so effective.

Sandler concluded that, to succeed on a sustainable basis, salespeople must observe these three simple rules:

- Engage with the most promising buyers – and filter out those unlikely to make a purchase.
- Foster the most productive conversations possible – by guiding a mutually beneficial discovery process that reveals the buyer's motivations, budget, and decision-making criteria.
- Secure the sale or move on – present your solution, obtain a decision, and avoid wasting time pursuing prospects who are not ready to buy.

Delving Deeper in The Sandler Way

You may not have realised it, but at the outset of every sales relationship, you have a choice to make. You can either integrate into the buyer's process or invite the buyer to engage with yours. Over time, through exposure to countless sales pitches, buyers have become adept at navigating the selling landscape, often undermining it to their advantage. They wield a surprisingly limited yet effective arsenal of tactics to take control and swiftly derail sales efforts.

STEP 1: BUYERS KEEP THEIR CARDS CLOSE TO THEIR CHEST

Typically, buyers reveal very little about their circumstances or intentions. They're unlikely to discuss budget or share insights into how they will decide whether to purchase your solution or which competitors they might be considering.

Consider a game of poker. What would you do if someone leaned over and asked, "Before I raise the bet, can I see your cards?" Instinctively, you would pull your cards closer to you.

Buyers are keen to prevent salespeople from gaining any perceived advantage by revealing information about their circumstances. They are safeguarding themselves against overzealous sales tactics and resisting manipulation of their wants and needs. Even well-meaning individuals often feel free to say whatever they like to salespeople. When communicating through digital platforms like text or email, which offer a sense of anonymity, they may be even more inclined to stretch the truth.

It is important to note however, that they don't mislead you because they're inherently bad; rather, it's a matter of self-preservation. After all, buyers are well aware that while they're preoccupied with their own affairs, you're honing your skills at workshops designed to turn you into an exceptional salesperson. They understand that you're learning how to guide them towards making purchasing decisions, and they worry about being outsmarted by a slick, savvy seller. With every new sales encounter, they become a touch more astute as your competitors exhaust the same age-old closing techniques.

Buyers recognise that one of your primary objectives is to spark interest in what you offer. Consequently, they may either dismiss you outright to rid themselves of the conversation quickly, or they might feign interest to extract information. A buyer may begin with comments like, "We've heard fantastic things about your company's ability to…" or "We'd like to understand how you can assist us with…" They might even claim their current solution is working perfectly well, when in reality, it's in disarray.

Meanwhile, they will share as little information as possible about their true circumstances or intentions. They'll give no indication of just how much they really need your solution. They won't divulge specific details about their budget or how they make purchasing decisions. It's crucial to recognise that the information a buyer offers is often incomplete.

Bear in mind, you're not the first salesperson your buyer has encountered. You may be an excellent, genuine professional with a fantastic opportunity to present. However, your buyer doesn't know this yet. They see you as just another typical "salesperson," complete with all the negative connotations that title carries.

STEP 2: THE BUYER WANTS TO KNOW WHAT YOU KNOW

This would be encouraging if the buyer were willing to pay for your insights. Instead, they're after information for free. Why? Because you are a professional! You possess knowledge about potential solutions that they lack.

Your buyer assumes that you have the ability to enhance their life or business. After all, why would your company put in the effort to bring your products and services to the marketplace otherwise?

The buyer believes you excel at what you do and that you hold something of value. They aim to extract your expertise and secure your best price, but not necessarily because they intend to make a purchase. They might be looking to use your pricing as leverage against a current supplier. They may need your figures to tell their boss or your competitors, "I've found a better price than what you're offering."

Believe it or not, there are numerous salespeople out there eager to provide disingenuous buyers with as much free information and competitive pricing as they can handle. This behaviour undermines the marketplace, transforming valuable solutions into ruthless commodities.

You may remember that we refer to this type of selling as "unpaid consulting". As you can imagine, the long-term prospects for unpaid consultants are rather bleak. Each year, many salespeople retire early when they realise that unpaid consulting doesn't put food on the table. It's the buyer's system that exploits the salesperson.

STEP 3: THE BUYER COMMITS TO NOTHING

Even after your buyer has secured the pricing or information they were after, they might not be finished with you just yet. They could require a little more "unpaid" effort on your part, leading you to believe that a sale is just around the corner. They dangle the tantalising prospect of a deal in front of you, saying things like:

"I need to give it some thought."

"Can you confirm all that in writing and I'll come back to you"

"This is quite intriguing. I'd like to present it to the committee."

"We're considering forming a project team to assess the feasibility…"

"Give me a ring after the holidays. Oh, not those holidays—I meant the next ones."

Typically, they'll hold out just enough hope to continue to string you along as a willing and subservient unpaid consultant. You're walking around saying, "Yes, I've got a great lead here, this is going to be my pay-day" when chances are you have nothing. Eventually, when your buyer has all the free information they need from you, as far as they're concerned, the process, AKA The Buyer-Seller Dance, is over.

STEP 4: THE BUYER DISAPPEARS

Before you know it, you find yourself being ghosted, left hanging by unanswered voicemail and emails. Your connection has been cut, but you remain oblivious, as no one has bothered to inform you. Meanwhile, you persist in following up, adhering to what you've been taught. You're trapped, clinging to the hope that there's still a chance for a sale. Yet, the truth is, the deal is already dead; you just haven't come to terms with it, having invested so much time and effort pursuing this elusive opportunity.

It doesn't help that the deal is already logged in the CRM system; everyone has seen the pipeline numbers and sales forecasts. This only makes it harder to let go of the opportunity. Does this sound familiar? Is this an uncomfortable truth?

Unless you have a solid plan to break free from the patterns of typical salespeople, establish equal standing in business discussions, and lead a collaborative sales process, your buyer will exploit this system and take the lead by default. You'll find yourself caught in a game you simply cannot win.

So, why do buyers play this game? **Because it works for them!**

TYPICAL SELLING SYSTEMS

Many sales training programmes adhere to traditional methods that often dictate how salespeople should engage with customers. These guidelines typically encourage practices such as:

- Emphasising features and benefits
- Relying heavily on presentation skills to close the sale
- Withholding essential information—such as pricing and terms—until a sense of "value" is established
- Anticipating and addressing buyer hesitations and objections
- Constantly pushing for closure using an array of tried-and-tested closing techniques

This approach, while somewhat conventional, can yield results from time to time, which explains its longevity. However, it often leads salespeople to keep rolling the dice, hoping for success rather than relying on a genuine connection. It's crucial to recognise that people make purchases in spite of these tactics, not because of them.

In today's world, where the modern, informed buyer has access to a wealth of information at their fingertips, these outdated sales techniques are becoming increasingly ineffective. Sadly, the most aggressive, manipulative, and high-pressure strategies still persist, fostering a confrontational dynamic with buyers and tarnishing the reputation of the sales profession.

If you use a traditional sales approach, chances are buyers don't like it, you don't get a deep understanding of your prospect's real needs, and your repeat business or loyalty is relatively poor. In other words, you've become a drain without knowing it.

Here are some of the most common reasons why:

- While you might be promoting features and benefits, it's essential to recognise that people don't actually purchase those—they seek solutions to their problems.
- If you lean too heavily on your presentation skills to secure the deal, you might invest considerable time and effort into a sales call, only to find that the necessary interest was never there.
- Delaying the discussion of price and terms until the end of the sales process could lead to wasted time on unqualified prospects, leaving you with dead-end opportunities.
- When you concentrate solely on addressing objections, you create a negotiation dynamic where the buyer often adopts a negative stance, voicing only reasons why your solution won't work.
- Lastly, your conventional closing techniques are likely familiar to your buyer. Strategies like the "Impending Event" or "Alternate Choice" closes have lost their effectiveness and no longer hold the same sway.

The buyer's system and the stereotypical sales system are now in sync... is the perfect match: the salesperson is looking for interested buyers; the buyers are seeking free consulting; they find each other, and the connection is made.

The buyer wants information, prices, proposals, drawings, projections, and more, and the salesperson is all too glad to get a willing dance partner after getting so many other rejections. The salesperson finally gets a chance to give their best pitch, and the two are dancing beautifully together.

Perhaps now it's time to shift your focus and connect with buyers in a way that truly resonates with their needs and concerns.

The Sandler Way

To achieve consistent success in sales where you don't turn into an unwilling drain, you need a selling system that dismantles the usual patterns of buying and selling. The Sandler Selling System offers a straightforward, no-nonsense approach that transforms the sales call into a business meeting between equals. This method focuses on strategically building trust, establishing a mutually beneficial arrangement, qualifying buyers as ideal clients, showcasing a unique value proposition that aligns with their needs, and solidifying the agreement.

In the Sandler system, the salesperson takes on the role of a highly skilled business consultant. Rather than subjecting your buyer to yet another generic sales pitch, you engage in an honest, non-manipulative exchange of information. The result is a refreshing and disarming experience that fosters genuine connections.

The guiding principles behind the Sandler Selling System are simple:

- Professional selling is a noble profession. Do not let the buyer treat you with disrespect.
- Be sure to understand the buyer's needs, budget, and decision making process before you try to sell them anything.
- Help the buyer discover the real reasons for their problem—and that you are the solution.

There are seven steps to achieving this, sometimes called the Sandler Submarine (more on that after this section). Here's a brief overview:

STEP 1: STOP ACTING LIKE A SALESPERSON & BUILD RAPPORT INSTEAD

When buyers sense that you're trying to sell them something, they often put up a protective "wall." At this juncture, your goal is to make the buyer feel at ease and demonstrate that you're not like the average salesperson. Show them that you truly understand their concerns from their perspective. Start to forge a connection and consistently nurture that rapport and trust throughout the entire sales journey, not just in those initial moments.

STEP 2: ESTABLISH AN UP-FRONT CONTRACT

Before every cricket match, the umpire gathers the managers from both teams at the pitch. They discuss the rules of the game, covering the boundaries, the wickets, and any peculiarities specific to that particular ground. For instance, when a batsman hits the ball off the wicketkeeper's helmet and it lands in the netting behind, there's no doubt that it's a no-ball. Similarly, when the batsman sends the ball soaring over the boundary and into the stands, it's clearly a six. Imagine the chaos that could arise if the managers and the umpire didn't agree in advance on the ground rules for the match!

At Sandler, this crucial step is referred to as the Up-Front Contract; a verbal agreement of what's going to happen and possible outcomes, one of which is always *not* working together, this resets the buyers mindset. It creates a mutual understanding between the salesperson and the buyer regarding what each party can expect from the sales process. These ground rules define behavioural boundaries, decision-making steps, and the necessary actions needed to meet those expectations. It's also important to seek permission to engage the buyer and outline the agenda for the meeting. When both parties agree at the outset to interact openly, they can feel more secure and avoid any potential misunderstandings as they begin to build their relationship.

Keep in mind that your sales approach will likely differ from what they anticipate. People are less likely to put up defensive barriers when they feel secure and are aware of what to expect.

STEP 3: UNCOVER AND PROBE YOUR BUYER'S "PAIN"

Before anything else, it's essential to identify whether your buyers have a problem or pain that you can address, whether they genuinely want it resolved, and if they see you as the one to help them. If not, it's time to move on for the moment.

The most intense emotion people feel is pain. If your buyer is free from pain, securing a sale will be challenging. People tend to stick with what they know until the discomfort of remaining in their current situation outweighs the apprehension of embracing something new.

If you don't learn how to uncover your buyer's pain, you'll find yourself relying on the outdated principle of averages. Many salespeople aim simply to present their pitch and then attempt to close the sale. The Sandler Selling System® changes all that. Your new objective is to reveal the buyer's pain. Understanding why people choose to buy is crucial!

STEP 4: TALK ABOUT MONEY

For many of us, this is the hardest step of all. Talking money isn't easy, we're taught at a young age not to probe into people finances but this is a crucial step. It's important tio remember that this isn't just about your cost of goods or services but also the cost to the buyer if you do nothing. If you can't fix their pain points, what might that actually cost the buyers business in losses?

There will be key questions here:

- What is the financial impact of the issues (pain) you have uncovered?
- Do they have the budget, time, and resources necessary for you to fix their problem?
- What happens if they don't take action (amplifying the pain)?
- And are they willing to invest in a solution for this problem?

Step 4 can be significantly more complex than simply asking, "Do they you the funds?" Consideration of time and resources can also be key disqualifiers. Do they possess the time, information, or other necessary conditions required to resolve their issue? If they don't, then they won't be suitable for your services.

It's essential to address this step prior to making a presentation, ensuring that you can receive proper compensation for your efforts.

STEP 5: UNCOVER YOUR BUYER'S DECISION-MAKING PROCESS

It's vital to grasp the buyer's decision-making process so you can position your solution as the clear choice. Does the individual you're engaging with possess the authority to make decisions? Consider how, when, where, and why they will arrive at their conclusion. Do they decide independently, or do they consult a colleague, partner, or committee? Will they take their time to reflect, or can they make a decision on the spot? Are they genuinely prepared to invest the necessary funds and resources to alleviate their pain?

If the answers to these questions are favourable and the odds are stacked in your favour, proceed with the process. If not, it's best to halt and disqualify them—just close the file. Only when you know that the buyer has a problem you can solve, along with a suitable budget, and you understand the who, where, when, why, what, and how of their decision-making, crafting a proposal they'll accept should be straightforward.

Remember, in this new approach, your presentation should focus less on the features and benefits of your business. Instead, it should centre on demonstrating how your solution can alleviate *their* pain. People don't purchase features and benefits; they invest in solutions to avoid or overcome discomfort.

STEP 6: FULFILMENT - THE SOLUTION TO SOLVE YOUR BUYER'S PAIN

Naturally, with this new approach, your presentation is less about the features and benefits that the marketing team has become enamoured with, and more about demonstrating to your buyer how your solution alleviates their pain points. After all, people don't purchase features; they invest in solutions that help them avoid or overcome discomfort.

This crucial stage, known as Fulfilment, is where you present that solution and secure the sale. While many sales training programmes refer to this part of the process as the presentation, it could equally be a proposal or even a casual conversation, depending on what aligns best with your buyer's decision-making process and your organisation's sales strategy.

A key aspect of the Sandler sales methodology is to ease the pressure surrounding the presentation. If we've implemented the system correctly up to this point, Fulfilment should simply serve as a confirmation of the agreements established along the way. This isn't about delivering a high-pressure performance in the hope of stumbling upon a reason for the customer to buy. Instead, there should be a mutual agreement for the buyer to decide, either way, at the conclusion of this step, without any pressure or tactics designed to manipulate their decision.

The momentum for closing the sale—or deciding to walk away—should be driven by the buyer's needs and their urgency to solve their problem. Your presentations ought to elicit a chorus of YES's, a few NO's, and nothing in between—no stalls, objections, or prolonged deliberations. If you encounter anything in between, it's likely a sign that trust wasn't sufficiently established, or that adequate discovery didn't occur earlier in the sales process. Late-stage objections can often indicate that a crucial element of qualification was overlooked.

STEP 7: REINFORCE THE SALE WITH A POST-SELL CONVERSATION

When most salespeople get a "yes," they grab the Purchase Order or contract and get out before anything goes wrong. That doesn't make the new client feel appreciated, it doesn't prepare them for the transition they're about to experience, and it doesn't do anything to keep them from the dreaded 'buyer's remorse'.

At this stage, you can also deal with any unresolved issues (like existing suppliers, TUPE issues or PR). If you hang in there for a few more minutes, a lot of potential problems can be avoided. This strategy will also firmly separate you from those stereotypical salespeople and position you as a trusted consultant rather than a preferred supplier.

The Sandler Submarine

To remember these important 7 steps for this proven process of managing leads, Sandler offers the submarine diagram. Why a submarine? Each compartment needs to be watertight before opening the hatch and progressing to the next compartment otherwise it's disaster!

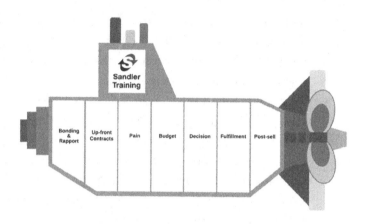

A Sandler Summary

Sandler has meticulously curated timeless success principles drawn from best practices worldwide over the past 50 years, refreshing them for today's fiercely competitive and intricate sales landscape. The insights shared here have empowered millions of sales professionals to elevate their careers. They employ the Sandler methodology, strategies, tools, and tactics daily, across virtually every industry, thriving in all economic climates.

The primary objectives for sales teams embracing these principles to enhance performance typically encompass:

- Increased Confidence in Selling: Cultivate a sales mindset and toolkit that quickly equips you with the expertise to establish credibility at the highest levels by building rapport, setting meeting agendas, and clarifying expectations for the sales process.

- Identifying Non-Buyers Early: Master the art of qualifying your prospects based on whether their needs, budget, and decision-making processes warrant your efforts in proposing a solution.

- Accelerated Sales Cycle: Create a clear, step-by-step sales plan that guides the process towards a timely and mutually agreeable outcome.

- Reduced Discounting: Gain the confidence and skills to shift the buyer's focus from the price of your solution to the cost of not implementing it, highlighting their return on investment by addressing their challenges.

- Higher Average Sales Value: Build the confidence, patience, and control necessary to conduct thorough needs analyses and budget discussions before proposing any solution.

- Improved Relationships: Foster a climate of trust and respect by utilising a sales methodology that sets you apart from the stereotypical, pushy salesperson. Truly understanding your buyer, their challenges, and their vision is far more impactful than merely showcasing your product knowledge.

- Effective Management of Complex Deals: Learn how to adeptly navigate situations involving multiple decision-makers from various departments, external consultants, committees, and other unexpected participants.

- Enhanced Closing Ratios in Competitive Environments: Differentiate yourself and your solution through a deep understanding of your buyer's needs and the precise execution of the

Sandler methodology, allowing you to compete effectively against incumbent vendors and other providers.

- **Reduced Cost Per Sale:** With more precise qualification of prospective buyers, allocate your valuable resources more judiciously. Say goodbye to free consulting.

- **More Cohesive Team Selling:** Experience the power of a sales team where every member understands and executes the same sales process, language, and methodology—ensuring every interaction propels the deal forward.

- **Accurate Forecasting:** Achieve significant milestones throughout the sales process and enhance the qualification of opportunities, leading to a more reliable projection of deals with a significantly reduced margin of error.

- **Increased Activity Levels per Salesperson:** Implement clearly defined tactics and strategies that yield victories on a minute-by-minute basis.

- **Enhanced Internal Communication:** Ensure that all conversations impacting your sales cycle are more productive, regardless of who is involved.

- **Overall Boost in Employee Engagement:** Enjoy heightened engagement and lower turnover, as employees feel positive about themselves, their organisation, and the marketplace.

Tips for Business and Life:

Embrace the Sandler way, reference the submarine, and be ruthless about your prospecting process. In our experience the hardest part for any business owner is burning your bridges of hope; in other words, letting go of those prospects that are stringing you along, getting free consultancy with the promise of project work to come and ultimately sapping your energy. Swapping these for prospects who offer a more mutually respectful conversation about wants and needs without the drawn out 'buyer-seller dance' is energising.

If you are considering adopting this pioneering sales process within your team or business, here are some tips and hints that will help:

1. Understand the Framework: Familiarise yourself with the key stages of The Sander Sales Process, ensuring your team comprehends the methodology and its benefits.

2. Invest in Training: Provide comprehensive training for your sales team to effectively implement the process. Consider workshops and role-playing exercises to reinforce learning.

3. Customise to Your Needs: Adapt the process to fit your specific industry and customer base. Tailoring the approach can enhance relevance and effectiveness.

4. Focus on Building Relationships: Emphasise the importance of establishing rapport with potential clients (the first compartment of the Sandler

Submarine). A relationship-driven approach can lead to greater trust and sales success.

5. Utilise Technology: Leverage CRM systems to track interactions and manage leads efficiently. This will streamline the sales process and improve communication.

6. Monitor Progress: Regularly review performance metrics to assess the effectiveness of the sales process. Adjust strategies as necessary to improve outcomes.

7. Encourage Feedback: Foster an environment where team members feel comfortable providing feedback on the process. Continuous improvement can lead to better results.

8. Don't be a Drain: If you recognise those drain-like behaviours in yourself or others, point them out and be more radiant in your approach; this book has equipped you with those skills.

9. Celebrate Successes: Recognise and reward achievements within your sales team to motivate and encourage adherence to the new process.

XIII A FINAL WORD FROM THE AUTHORS

We hope you enjoyed reading this book as much as we did writing it. It's been a learning experience for us as we dived into the complexities behind those Drains and Radiator labels, challenging your assumptions and helping you see beyond the obvious. We hope that you feel more empowered in spotting the fakers, uncovering the real radiators, and now know how to steer clear of the drains that can sabotage your success and disrupt your quality of life and peace of mind.

But we'd like to leave you with a final thought before you embark on your own journey of discovery to elevate both your personal and professional life by surrounding yourself with true radiators of success: *People can't radiate if their bosses drain them, leaving with nothing to radiate with.*

When individuals cannot express their full potential, creativity, or positivity because they they are overworked, undervalued, or emotionally depleted by their leaders, they naturally become drains. We all have the ability to radiate, to shine, share energy, or contribute positively to our environment but if our bosses or managers consistently demand too much without providing support, recognition, or encouragement, employees inevitably feel exhausted and demotivated.

This behaviour leads to a lack of enthusiasm and creativity... you literally feel drained. Essentially, for people to thrive and contribute meaningfully, they need to be nurtured and supported rather than drained and so this book acts as a self-help guide for those that are ready to acknowledge that sometimes, they push too hard.

We'll leave the final words to an inspirational quote from Mahatma Ghandi:

"Carefully watch your thoughts, for they become your words. Manage and watch your words, for they will become your actions. Consider and judge your actions, for they have become your habits. Acknowledge and watch your habits, for they shall become your values. Understand and embrace your values, for they become your destiny."

XIV

CREDIT AND REFERENCES

Acknowledgement to many people who contributed

nterviewer, Adam Jacques of The Independent and his 2011 interview with Dave Steward

Researcher, Jennifer E. Lansford, PhD, a professor with the Social Science Research Institute and the Centre for Child and Family Policy at Duke University.

Dr Andy Cope, a happiness expert, positive psychologist and author of The Art of Being Brilliant.

Author Elisabeth Kübler-Ross 1969 book On Death and Dying and the subsequent adaptation into the Kübler-Ross change curve

American psychologist Abraham Maslow for his original 1943 paper "A Theory of Human Motivation" and subsequent Maslow's Hierarchy of Needs

US Magazine Psychology Today who featured Friendship Doctor Irene S Levine Ph.D. and published My Friend Is Draining Me! In 2013

Akyalcin, E., Greenway, P., & Miln, L. (2008). Measuring transcendence: Extracting core constructs. The Journal of Transpersonal Psychology, 40(1), 41–59.

Ackerman, J. & Kenrick, D. T. (2009). Cooperative courtship: Helping friends raise and raze relationship barriers: How men and women cooperate in courtship. Personality & Social Psychology Bulletin, 35, 1285–1300.

Crawford, C., & Krebs, D. (2008). Foundations of evolutionary psychology. Erlbaum.

Collier, L. (2016). Growth after trauma. Monitor on Psychology, 47(10), 48.

Dunbar, R. I. M., & Barrett, L. (2007). Oxford handbook of evolutionary psychology. Oxford University Press.

Freund, K. S., & Lous, J. (2012). The effect of preventive consultations on young adults with psychosocial problems: a randomized trial. Health Education Research, 27(5), 927–945.

Griskevicius, V., Cialdini, R. B., & Kenrick, D. T. (2006). Peacocks, Picasso, and parental investment: The effects of romantic motives on creativity. Journal of Personality and Social Psychology, 91, 63–76.

Kaufman, S. B. (2019, April 23). Who created Maslow's iconic pyramid? Scientific American. https://blogs.scientificamerican.com/beautiful-minds/who-created-maslows-iconic-pyramid/.

Kenrick, D. T., Griskevicius, V., Neuberg, S. L., & Schaller, M. (2010). Renovating the pyramid of needs: Contemporary extensions built upon ancient foundations. Perspectives on Psychological Science, 5(3), 292–314.

Koltko-Rivera, M. E. (2006). Rediscovering the later version of Maslow's hierarchy of needs: Self-transcendence and opportunities for theory, research, and unification. Review of General Psychology, 10(4), 302–317.

Maslow, A. H. (1943). A theory of human motivation. Psychological Review, 50, 370–396.

Maslow, A. H. (1970). Motivation and personality (2nd ed.). Harper & Row.

Moitra, M., Owens, S., Hailemariam, M., Wilson, K. S., Mensa-Kwao, A., Gonese, G., Kamamia, C. K., White, B., Young, D. M., & Collins, P. Y. (2023). Global mental health: Where we are and where we are going. Current Psychiatry Reports, 25(7), 301–311.

Munroe, M., & Ferrari, M. (Eds.). (2022). Posttraumatic growth to psychological well-being: Coping wisely with adversity. Springer.

Ryu, S., & Fan, L. (2023). The relationship between financial worries and psychological distress among U.S. adults. Journal of Family and Economic Issues, 44(1), 16–33.

Tay, L., & Diener, E. (2011). Needs and subjective well-being around the world. Journal of Personality and Social Psychology, 101(2), 354–365.

Ronald Reagan's great quote: "It's hard, when you're up to your armpits in alligators, to remember you came here to drain the swamp."

Walt Whitman 'Keep your face always toward the sunshine - and shadows will fall behind you.'

Emily Frieze-Kemeny, CEO and Founder of AROSE Group, a leadership consulting firm that bridges humanity and profitability.

The Richer Way by Julian Richer for being the first business book I ever read from cover to cover.

Professor Steve Peters, a specialist in the functioning of the human mind, founder of charitable company Chimp Management for his working on The Chimp Management Mind Model

Harvard Business Publishing, an affiliate of Harvard Business School, and their study of direct reports and business leaders in 2015

Business Insider interview with Patrick O'Neill, who left his job at TBWA/Chiat/Day, the ad agency where he was a creative director, to work alongside disgraced Theranos CEO Elizabeth Holmes.

Dr Allison Gaffey at Yale Medicine's Department of Internal Medicine, for her insights on addressing the impacts of stress.

Remez Sasson and Kendra Cherry from Very Well Mind for their definitions of Positive Mental Attitude

Ron Gutman, the author of Smile: The Astonishing Powers of a Simple Act

David H. Sandler for his robust professional sales methodology, The Sandler Way and his innovative diagram The Sandler Submarine.

Thanks to that inspirational quote from Mahatma Ghandi "Carefully watch your thoughts"